Cambridge Elements ≡

Elements in Philosophy of Science
edited by
Jacob Stegenga
University of Cambridge

CLIMATE SCIENCE

Wendy S. Parker
Virginia Tech

CAMBRIDGE
UNIVERSITY PRESS

Shaftesbury Road, Cambridge CB2 8EA, United Kingdom

One Liberty Plaza, 20th Floor, New York, NY 10006, USA

477 Williamstown Road, Port Melbourne, VIC 3207, Australia

314–321, 3rd Floor, Plot 3, Splendor Forum, Jasola District Centre,
New Delhi – 110025, India

103 Penang Road, #05–06/07, Visioncrest Commercial, Singapore 238467

Cambridge University Press is part of Cambridge University Press & Assessment,
a department of the University of Cambridge.

We share the University's mission to contribute to society through the pursuit of
education, learning and research at the highest international levels of excellence.

www.cambridge.org
Information on this title: www.cambridge.org/9781009619349

DOI: 10.1017/9781009619301

First published 2024

A catalogue record for this publication is available from the British Library

ISBN 978-1-009-61934-9 Hardback
ISBN 978-1-009-61931-8 Paperback
ISSN 2517-7273 (online)
ISSN 2517-7265 (print)

Climate Science

Elements in Philosophy of Science

DOI: 10.1017/9781009619301
First published online: December 2024

Wendy S. Parker
Virginia Tech

Author for correspondence: Wendy S. Parker, wendyparker@vt.edu

Abstract: This Element examines how climate scientists have arrived at answers to three key questions about climate change: How much is Earth's climate warming? What is causing this warming? What will climate be like in the future? Resources from philosophy of science are employed to analyse the methods that climate scientists use to address these questions and the inferences that they make from the evidence collected. Along the way, the analysis contributes to broader philosophical discussions of data modelling and measurement, robustness analysis, explanation, and model evaluation.

Keywords: climate science, computer simulation, evidence, robustness, measurement

ISBNs: 9781009619349 (HB), 9781009619318 (PB), 9781009619301 (OC)
ISSNs: 2517-7273 (online), 2517-7265 (print)

Contents

1 Introduction

In the first half of the twentieth century, the study of earth's climate was known as "climatology" and was mainly a descriptive endeavor. Pioneering work of the nineteenth century had developed systems for classifying regional climates as well as explanations for broad variations in climate around the globe (Weart 2023). By the mid twentieth century, however, the work of climatologists consisted chiefly in compiling data about weather conditions in regions of interest and deriving statistics, often with an eye to applications in agriculture and engineering (Weart 2023). Climatology was more akin to geography than to physics.

In contrast, climate science today takes as its object of study a complex dynamical system, *earth's climate system*, encompassing the atmosphere, oceans, land surface, ice sheets, and even aspects of the biosphere. It seeks to understand the detailed workings of this dynamical system – how myriad physical, chemical, and biological processes jointly produce patterns of observed climate conditions and their changes over time – and to predict how the system will respond to interventions, such as increases or decreases in atmospheric greenhouse gas concentrations. In doing so, it makes extensive use of physical theory and computational modeling, alongside massive volumes of data from global observing networks.

This shift in practice was precipitated to a significant extent by the advent of digital computing. Starting in the 1950s, with the help of the computer, scientists were for the first time able to use fluid dynamical equations to simulate the atmosphere's general circulation, which distributes heat and moisture around the globe (see Phillips 1956). In the decades that followed, these general circulation models were expanded to include representations of many other processes that influence earth's near-surface climate: the transport of heat by ocean currents, the formation of clouds and precipitation, the evaporation of moisture from the land surface, the melting of reflective polar ice, and more. These global climate models became a central tool of climate research.

Much of this research has been directed at understanding *changes in climate* – changes in the statistical distribution of local, regional, or global weather conditions when considered over long time periods, such as several decades or longer. In the 1970s, understanding how and why past ice ages occurred was a major focus of investigation. More recently, anthropogenic climate change has dominated climate science's research agenda and has spurred dramatic growth and development of climate science as a field. For several decades, climate scientists have been intensely investigating not only the extent and causes of ongoing changes in global and regional climate but also more fundamental questions about the physical processes and feedbacks involved in such changes.

Understanding of the climate system and of climate change has advanced markedly as a result.

This progress is well documented in the periodic assessment reports of the U.N. Intergovernmental Panel on Climate Change (IPCC), an evolving body of thousands of volunteer scientific experts from around the world. Every 5–7 years since 1990, the IPCC has reviewed the latest research related to climate change and assessed its implications for a range of important questions, including questions about the extent and causes of ongoing climate change, the way climate might further change in the future, impacts of these changes on humans and the environment, and options for adapting to or mitigating climate change (see, e.g., IPCC 2023). Answers to many of these questions have grown increasingly clear over time, undergirding international policy agreements like the Kyoto Protocol and the Paris Agreement.

Climate science has also proven to be a rich site for philosophical analysis. In fact, it is fair to say that over the last decade a new subfield of philosophy of science has emerged: *the philosophy of climate science*. Work in this area has tended to focus on issues in the methodology and epistemology of climate modeling (e.g., Parker 2006; Lenhard and Winsberg 2010; Lloyd 2015; Dethier 2022; Kawamleh 2022), but increasingly a broad range of topics is being addressed – from the conceptual foundations of climate science (e.g., Werndl 2016; Katzav and Parker 2018), to the roles of non-epistemic values in climate science (e.g., Biddle and Winsberg 2010; Lloyd and Oreskes 2018; Pulkkinen et al. 2022; Elabbar 2023), to expert judgment in climate science (e.g., Thompson et al. 2016; Jebeile and Crucifix 2020; Lam and Majszak 2022), to methods of paleoclimate research (e.g., Vezér 2017; Wilson and Boudinot 2022; Watkins 2024), just to name a few.[1]

This Element is a contribution to the philosophy of climate science. It aims to advance the epistemology of climate science by examining how climate scientists have arrived at answers to three key questions about climate change:

➢ How much is earth's climate warming?
➢ What is causing this warming?
➢ What will climate be like in the future?

Resources from philosophy of science will be employed to analyze both the methods that climate scientists use in addressing these questions and the inferences that they make from the evidence collected. Along the way, the analysis will draw upon, and contribute to, broader philosophical discussions regarding

---

[1] Overviews of issues in philosophy of climate science include: Frigg et al. (2015a, 2015b), Parker (2018), Lloyd and Winsberg (2018), Winsberg (2018a), and Bradley et al. (2020).

data modeling and measurement, evidence, robustness analysis, explanation, and model evaluation.

The Element is divided into three main sections, each focused on one of the three key questions. These are followed by a brief concluding section that draws out some general features of the epistemology of climate science suggested by the analysis and then offers some reflections on future directions. The sections can be read independently but are best read in order.

How much is earth's climate warming? Section 2 examines how climate scientists infer long-term changes in global temperature from local thermometer data. It characterizes global temperature datasets as data models and argues that estimates of global temperature change derived from those datasets can be considered measurement outcomes. Jonah Schupbach's (2018) explanatory account of robustness analysis is employed to demonstrate the epistemic significance of the robustness of these temperature change estimates to variations in methods, data, and research teams. Finally, it is argued that, even from the perspective of a demanding account of evidence like Deborah Mayo's (1996, 2018) error-statistical account, there is good evidence that earth's climate has warmed significantly since the late nineteenth century.

What is causing this warming? Section 3 turns to climate scientists' efforts to explain recent warming. After identifying several obstacles to explanation in climate science, it highlights the use of computational models as bookkeeping devices – as presciently envisioned by atmospheric scientist Ed Lorenz (1970) – to make progress in the face of these obstacles. It also considers how headline conclusions about the causes of recent warming are reached by the IPCC and how philosophical theories of evidence might be applied in this context. A central thesis of this section is that computational modeling has played a crucial role in moving climate science beyond qualitative speculation about the causes of climate phenomena. Nevertheless, there are significant explanatory pitfalls to watch out for.

What will climate be like in the future? Section 4 discusses the use of ensembles of climate models to investigate, and to help gauge uncertainty about, future changes in climate. Inspired by practice in this context, it articulates a form of robustness analysis underwritten by jury theorem reasoning, which is distinct from Schupbach's explanatory variety. It then explains why climate science is beginning to move away from the practice of "model democracy" (Knutti 2010), where each state-of-the-art climate model's projection is given equal weight, and suggests that new methods for weighting projections align with a fitness-for-purpose perspective on model evaluation. It closes with an overview of recent discussions of the management of inductive risk in climate science.

2 Measuring Global Temperature Change

How much is earth's climate changing? Answering this question is far from simple, even when attention is limited to changes in a single, indicative climate variable: earth's average near-surface temperature, hereafter *global temperature*. There is no global thermometer from which scientists can simply read off the global temperature whenever desired. Instead, variations in global temperature are estimated by synthesizing a host of local temperature measurements that are distributed unevenly around the globe and that must be adjusted to account for jumps and trends that reflect non-climatic changes, such as replacing an instrument at an observing station or moving an instrument away from encroaching buildings or vegetation.[2] Nevertheless, climate scientists have reached some firm conclusions about global temperature change. The IPCC considers it "certain" that global temperature has increased since the late nineteenth century (Hartmann et al. 2013). In fact, analyses consistently find that average global temperature over the last decade was about 1°C warmer than in the late nineteenth century (see Gulev et al. 2021, Table 2.4).

This section examines how these analyses of global temperature change are produced and argues that they constitute good evidence of a significantly warming world, especially when considered in conjunction with other observations of the climate system. Section 2.1 gives an overview of the key steps involved in standard approaches to producing global temperature datasets and characterizes these datasets as *data models*. Section 2.2 calls attention to the robustness of estimates of global temperature change derived from these datasets and argues that these estimates can be considered *measurement outcomes*. Section 2.3 examines in more detail the evidential significance of this robustness. Finally, Section 2.4 argues that there is good evidence that earth's climate has warmed significantly since the late nineteenth century.

2.1 Making Data Global

To estimate changes in global temperature, researchers typically start with local thermometer readings made at weather stations on land and on ships and buoys at sea. Land stations report near-surface air temperature, while ocean data indicate the temperature of sea water collected near the surface. Nowadays, observations are made daily at thousands of locations around the globe. Going back in time, and especially prior to the mid twentieth century,

---

[2] For periods prior to the late nineteenth century, when networks of weather observing stations reached a critical mass, the task is even more difficult; for these periods, estimates of global temperature change are derived from patterns in tree rings, ice cores, and other proxy indicators for temperature.

observing networks become significantly sparser. Nevertheless, altogether an enormous amount of temperature data is available – around a billion individual surface observations made since the late nineteenth century. Obtaining these data, however, is only the first step; these many local observations need to be transformed somehow into information about global temperature. As Paul Edwards (2010) puts it, climate researchers need to *make data global*.

Because land and sea data are subject to different sources of error, they are processed separately. The basic steps of the processing nevertheless are similar. First, there is quality control. Observations that are judged to be obviously erroneous are discarded. The remaining data undergo a process of correction known as *homogenization*, which aims to remove jumps and trends in data that result from changes in observing instruments or methods (e.g., using a different sort of bucket for collecting sea water), or changes in the siting of an instrument (e.g., moving it from one side of a station to the other), or changes in the surrounding land use (e.g., a rural observing site becoming an urban one over time). Given the huge number of observations to be processed, quality control and homogenization are largely automated.

Next, data are converted from absolute temperatures to temperature *anomalies*. An anomaly is just a deviation from a reference value, such as the average temperature at the observing station or ocean region in question during a specified thirty-year period. By subtracting such a reference value from each temperature value for the location, a time series of absolute temperatures for the location (24.4°C, 24.6°C, 24.1°C, . . .) becomes a time series of anomalies (+0.1°C, +0.3°C, –0.2°C, . . .). The shift to anomalies is made for a number of reasons. In many land regions, the spatial correlation among temperature anomalies is found to be stronger than the correlation among absolute temperatures (Hansen and Lebedeff 1987). This makes anomalies a better choice when it comes to filling in large gaps between observing stations – gaps that sometimes span hundreds of kilometers or more. In addition, anomalies are less affected by systematic error; deviations from a local reference temperature will be the same even if a thermometer always reads 1°C too cold or too hot.[3]

Typically, both land and ocean data will also be *regularized* in space and time. Each observation will be associated with a particular time period – a specific day or month – and a particular area on a spatial grid, for example, a 2°latitude × 2° longitude box. Average anomalies for a given grid box during a particular time period will be calculated as a function of the data available for locations within

---

[3] For more discussion of the use of anomalies and ambiguity in the meaning of "surface air temperature" see https://data.giss.nasa.gov/gistemp/faq/abs_temp.html, accessed December 5, 2023. See also Thorne et al. (2021).

that grid box during that time period. Different research teams handle empty grid boxes differently, with some simply reporting that no data are available and others attempting to fill in gaps by spatial interpolation. Regularizing has a number of benefits. Gridding data helps to ensure that global averages aren't unduly influenced by areas where the density of observations is greater, and it puts the data into a convenient format for comparison with output from climate simulations. Temporal averaging smooths over short-term variability that isn't relevant for most climate research.

Global datasets are produced by conjoining these gridded land and sea datasets. Such datasets are often referred to as *data products* by climate scientists, to signal that their production involves substantial processing of data. In philosophers' terminology, they are *data models*. While the importance of data modeling in science was emphasized by Patrick Suppes (1962) decades ago, the practice of data modeling was largely neglected by philosophers until very recently. Today, there is increasing attention to the rich and varied practices of data modeling in science, as well as increasing emphasis on the representational function of data models: "Data models are ways of ordering data that are evaluated, manipulated and modified with the explicit goal of representing a phenomenon" (Leonelli 2019, p. 22; see also Harris 2003; van Fraassen 2008; Bokulich 2018; Bokulich and Parker 2021). A related but broader characterization will be adopted here: A *data model* is a representation of one or more aspects of the world, which is produced by processing data and/or other data models, in order to facilitate the achievement of scientific aims.

Data models can take the form of datasets, but they can take other forms too: graphs, charts, equations, and more. For example, Figure 1 is a data model that represents variation in global temperature since 1880. It was produced from a gridded global temperature dataset – GISTEMPv4 – by averaging regularized temperature anomalies from around the globe over each calendar year (squares) and applying a smoothing technique to make the longer-term trends easier to see (thicker line). Uncertainty ranges for the annual temperature anomaly estimates are shown as well (shading) (Lenssen et al. 2019). A major motivation for undertaking the hard work of producing gridded global temperature datasets is to be able to produce figures like Figure 1, which make it easier to see how global temperature has changed over time.

According to the characterization of data models adopted here, data models are both representations and intended to facilitate particular scientific aims. This suggests at least two perspectives that might be adopted when evaluating data models. On the first, a data model is of higher quality the closer it comes to representing targeted features of the world with perfect accuracy and at ultra-fine resolution. In effect, this view says that a data model is better the closer it

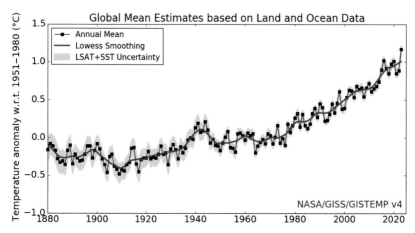

Figure 1 Estimates of global mean surface temperature variations from NASA GISS GISTEMPv4. (Source: NASA Goddard Institute for Space Studies, https://data.giss.nasa.gov/gistemp/graphs_v4/).

comes to *mirroring* a selected part of the world. A second approach focuses instead on the data model's *suitability for one or more purposes*. It asks whether the data model represents relevant aspects of the world sufficiently well, where what counts as relevant and sufficient depends on the purposes of interest, and it considers in addition whether nonrepresentational features of the data model – its format, portability, metadata, and so on – will facilitate or impede its use for those purposes. These considerations together inform a judgment about the data model's *adequacy* or *fitness* for the purpose at hand (Bokulich and Parker 2021).

While each of these views of data model quality has something to recommend it, there are reasons to prefer the second, fitness-for-purpose view. It can accommodate not only cases in which the data modeler's aim is purely representational but also cases in which a data model is constructed as a means to achieving other scientific aims, for example, to develop an explanation, answer a particular question, test a theory, communicate results, and so on. For the latter cases, the mirror view seems to miss the mark since, not infrequently, having a data model that closely approximates an ideal representation (i.e., one with extremely high fidelity and fine resolution) is neither necessary nor sufficient for successfully achieving a particular aim. Something far from the ideal might suffice, and nonrepresentational features such as format, manipulability, simplicity, etc. can be relevant. Of course, the fitness-for-purpose view does not deny that high-fidelity representation is usually desirable; it merely denies that more closely approximating an ideal representation is *always* more desirable and that representational fidelity is *all* that ever matters. If the goal is communicating findings or identifying patterns, for example, then the format of the data model might be especially important: Most people will get a better sense of how global temperature has warmed since the late nineteenth century by viewing Figure 1 than by examining a spreadsheet that contains the same annual temperature anomaly values and uncertainty ranges as a long list of numbers.

Clearly a data model that is adequate or fit for one purpose might fail to be so for another. Consider the dataset just mentioned: A spreadsheet providing an estimated global temperature anomaly, along with its 95 percent uncertainty interval, for each year since 1880, calculated from GISTEMPv4.[4] Because the uncertainty intervals for different years often overlap significantly (as is easily seen in Figure 1), a researcher taking this dataset at face value cannot use it for the purpose of (P_1) confidently ordering the years between 1880 and 2020 from hottest to coldest. On the other hand, the dataset might well be adequate for the purpose of (P_2) determining whether 2015 was hotter than 2000, since the uncertainty intervals for these two years do not come close to overlapping (see Figure 1). However, before concluding that the dataset is adequate for P_2 a researcher needs to consider how it was produced, including such things as: the spatial coverage of the underlying thermometer data for 2000 and 2015; how sources of error were corrected for (or not); how any spatial gaps were filled in; what assumptions were made when calculating uncertainty intervals; and so on. If, in light of this investigation, the researcher is convinced that major sources of error have been addressed and that uncertainties are unlikely to have been substantially underestimated, then she might conclude that the dataset is adequate for P_2 and that 2015 was hotter.

2.2 Data Models and Measurement

The standard approach to estimating changes in global temperature is the one outlined in the last section. But there are other approaches as well. For instance, some estimates of global temperature change are obtained via a process known as *data assimilation*, in which observational data and computer simulations are used together to estimate conditions. Data assimilation was first used in geophysics as a means of obtaining initial conditions for weather forecasting models. The basic idea is to take predictions from a simulation model as a first-guess estimate of weather conditions at time *t* and then adjust those estimated conditions in light of observations collected around time *t*, from thermometers, barometers, satellite-based radiometers, and so on. Because the simulation model predicts conditions for every model grid point, this method leaves no spatial gaps and, unlike simple

---

[4] Dataset available at https://data.giss.nasa.gov/gistemp/graphs_v4/, accessed October 31, 2023.

spatial interpolation, it employs not only observations collected around time *t* but also (implicitly) observations collected at earlier times, since the latter inform the initial conditions for the prediction that serves as the first guess.

There are several types of data assimilation method in use, which differ in how they perform the updating of the first-guess estimate. Some methods blend the forecast and observations for time *t*, giving some weight to each. Others iteratively search for an alternative forecast from the simulation model that better fits the available observations for *t* or for a window of time around *t*. In the context of weather prediction, the results of data assimilation serve as the initial conditions for the next forecast cycle and are known as an *analysis* for the forecast initialization time. In support of climate research, data assimilation is performed retrospectively: A past period, usually several decades or longer, is divided into a series of short windows (hours), and data assimilation is performed for each window using the same forecast model, generating a coherent time series of analyses of past conditions, which are known as *reanalyses* or *reanalysis datasets*. These reanalysis datasets are used for many purposes in climate research, including estimating changes in global temperature over time. For example, the ECMWF results shown in Figure 2 were calculated from the ERA-5 reanalysis, which provides hourly analyses of atmospheric conditions going back to 1940.[5]

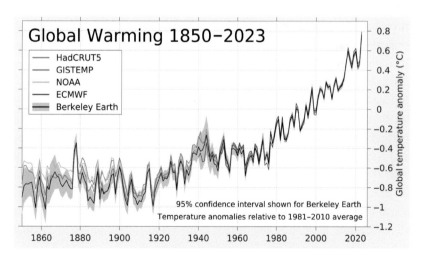

Figure 2 Time series of global surface temperature anomalies from several sources. (Source: Berkeley Earth, https://berkeleyearth.org/global-temperature-report-for-2023/. Reprinted with permission.).

---

[5] See https://www.ecmwf.int/en/forecasts/dataset/ecmwf-reanalysis-v5 for more details.

In fact, the curves in Figure 2 reflect *three* significantly different approaches to estimating global temperature change. The HADCRUT5, GISTEMP, and NOAA results were obtained by transforming local thermometer data into estimates of global temperature as discussed in Section 2.1, with variations in the range of data used, the corrections and homogenization algorithms employed, and the way gaps were treated. The ECMWF results were generated via reanalysis, as just explained. A third approach is represented by the Berkeley Earth results, whose production involved both a much more expansive set of thermometer data than was initially employed by HADCRUT5, GISTEMP, etc., and a quite different, geostatistical ("kriging") methodology for processing and synthesizing those data (Rohde et al. 2013). Yet despite these varied approaches, they all yield similar global temperature anomaly curves, with estimated uncertainties that are small compared to the temperature changes that they show over the period (see also Lenssen et al. 2019, Fig. 13). Put differently, the results shown in Figure 2 indicate that today's global temperature anomaly estimates exhibit a significant degree of *robustness*: Quite similar values are obtained from multiple investigations despite variations in researchers, underlying data, and methodologies.

Such robustness is a hallmark of successful *measurement*, according to contemporary philosophical accounts. For instance, Eran Tal (2012, 2017) articulates a robustness criterion that, when met, provides evidence of measurement accuracy under any of several understandings of accuracy. In essence, this robustness criterion requires (i) that discrepancies among outcomes from a sufficiently diverse set of procedures for estimating a quantity are statistically consistent with one another, given their respective uncertainties, and (ii) that those outcomes and uncertainties are derived in each case using an appropriate model of the measurement process, that is, one whose assumptions cohere well enough with what is known about the nature of the quantity under investigation and the particular realization of the procedure by which it was estimated. These criteria are reflected in Tal's characterization of measurement: To *measure* a physical quantity is to make coherent and consistent inferences from instrument indications to the value of a parameter in a model of the measurement process. The inferred value is the *measurement outcome* and should be accompanied by an indication of its associated uncertainty; measuring thus produces a *representation* of some aspect of the system under measurement.[6]

---

[6] van Fraassen (2008) articulates a view of measurement in which coherence and consistency play similar roles. His account too could be employed for the analysis that follows here, reaching similar conclusions.

The efforts of climate researchers to estimate global temperature anomalies fit Tal's picture rather well. Each of the three approaches (standard, reanalysis, and Berkeley Earth) involves inferring global temperature anomalies from instrument indications, where the inference is guided by a model of the measurement process. Consider first the standard and Berkeley Earth approaches. Here, the basic model of the measurement process is relatively simple: It assumes that thermometer indications can provide information about local temperature changes, which can be aggregated to estimate global changes. Complications arise as researchers choose which stations and readings to include in the analysis and try to account for the ways the actual measurement process deviates from the idealized basic model: to correct for interfering factors, to fill in gaps, and so on. The different groups make somewhat different choices, in part because there is uncertainty about which choices are best, but at least rough coherence with background knowledge is required. As illustrated in Figure 2, global temperature anomaly estimates produced in these different ways usually fall within each other's 95 percent uncertainty intervals or come close to doing so. In recent years, the methods for generating such uncertainty intervals have become substantially more thorough and rigorous, for example, by representing sources of uncertainty statistically and combining them via a formal uncertainty model (see e.g., Lenssen et al. 2019; Morice et al. 2021), as discussed further in Section 2.4.

What about efforts to derive global temperature anomaly estimates from reanalyses like ERA-5, where the reanalysis results consist of simulation output? Here, the model of the measurement process is substantially more complex: It includes assumptions not just about the indications of observing instruments like thermometers, barometers and radiometers, but also about the reliability of a weather forecasting model and about how to find better forecasts via an assimilation algorithm (Parker 2017). Some of these assumptions are known to be simplified and idealized in ways that are difficult to correct for in a principled way. In part because of this, it is more difficult to provide well-motivated uncertainty estimates for reanalysis results, and uncertainty information is sometimes not provided at all. Yet, in many cases, global temperature anomalies derived from reanalyses do agree closely with estimates produced via other methods. A reasonable conclusion is that investigations of global temperature change via reanalysis are at least attempts at measurement. Moreover, in principle, estimates of quantities produced via data assimilation methods, or involving simulation in other substantive roles, *can* be measurement outcomes; there is no in principle reason that a process embedding simulation couldn't satisfy Tal's robustness criterion for successful measurement (see also Parker 2021).

Such a conclusion – that even reanalysis results consisting of simulation output could be measurement outcomes – is less radical than it might initially seem. Metrologists already recognize that computer simulation can play various roles in measurement practices, and even a brief survey of contemporary science reveals a spectrum of "measuring" and "observing" practices that embed theoretical calculation and modeling to various degrees. Focusing just on meteorology and climate science one finds: Estimates of temperature and pressure from thermometer and barometer readings, involving no calculation; estimates of relative humidity involving simple theoretical calculation from wet bulb and dry bulb thermometer readings; estimates of storm motion using radar, where the observing system embeds theoretical Doppler effect calculations; and atmospheric temperature profiles derived from satellite-based radiometer data, which requires not only transforming from one physical variable to another but also solving an inverse problem. Data assimilation and reanalysis might occupy the far end of the spectrum of practices aimed at measuring quantities of interest, but they have nearby neighbors.

Reflecting on Tal's account of measurement, we find a close connection between measurement and data modeling. A measurement outcome *just is* a data model in the sense articulated earlier: It is a representation of one or more aspects of the world, which is produced by processing data and/or other data models (themselves derived from instrument indications), in order to facilitate the achievement of some scientific aim – in this case, to accurately estimate the value of a quantity. With this in mind, we can also characterize somewhat differently one approach to evaluating the adequacy-for-purpose of data models produced for measurement purposes: The evaluation involves, in part, *systematically scrutinizing a model of a measurement process*. What are its assumptions? Are they well-motivated? How does the actual measuring process deviate from this idealized model? How have these deviations been accounted for? And so on. Answers to these questions can warrant greater confidence that the data model generated via the measurement process is adequate (or not) for the purpose of interest.

2.3 The Significance of Robustness

Tal's robustness criterion for successful measurement requires *sufficient diversity* among the procedures used to estimate quantity values. He does not say what counts as sufficiently diverse, though. Presumably, simply repeating the same measurement procedure is insufficient, and presumably the more diverse the procedures the better. Yet even characterizing what counts as *more diverse* is not so straightforward. Philosophers as well as scientists have disagreed about this in broader discussions of the evidential value of robust results in science.

Oftentimes, some notion of independence is invoked, but there is disagreement over how that notion should be understood as well and, in some cases of robustness, a focus on independence of any sort seems misplaced or inapt.

Recently, Jonah Schupbach (2018) has attempted to remedy the situation by offering an explanatory account of robustness, which is meant to apply generally. He argues that results from multiple investigations enhance support for a hypothesis H that explains those results when some of the results *rule out alternatives to H* that would otherwise be left standing. To see the basic idea, imagine a simple case where there is agreement among a set of results ($r_1 \ldots r_m$), which could be explained by hypothesis H or by either of two competing hypotheses, H' and H''. On Schupbach's account, a new result, r_n, adds relevant diversity to the set of agreeing results, and enhances support for H, when it helps to rule out one of those competing explanations of agreement among ($r_1 \ldots r_m$). For example, perhaps only H and H'', but not H', can explain ($r_1 \ldots r_n$). While Schupbach's account does not tell us what counts as *sufficiently* diverse estimation procedures, such that we can claim to successfully measure a quantity, it does help us to evaluate whether a result from an additional procedure *enhances* (or provides incremental) support for a hypothesis, whether the hypothesis is about the value of a quantity or something else.

We can use Schupbach's account to see that the agreement among global temperature analyses like those shown in Figure 2 is evidentially significant. Suppose a scientific hypothesis that interests us is (H_{1C}) *average global temperature in the year 2020 was more than 1.0°C warmer than average global temperature during the period 1880–1899.* Each of the standard analyses in Figure 2 (HADCRUT5, GISTEMP, and NOAA) gives a result that accords with H_{1C}. One possible explanation for this agreement among the standard analyses is that H_{1C} is true, and each of the standard analyses proceeded in a way that accurately (enough) estimated the change in temperature. But there are other possible explanations too. For example, some climate contrarians have proposed hypotheses like:

(H') Agreement among warming estimates from standard analyses stems from a shared reliance on land-based thermometer data that are biased by urban heat island effects, poor station siting and other problems; the actual warming is much less.

Another possible explanation is:

(H'') The agreement among warming estimates from standard analyses stems from shared biases in homogenization efforts, such as a tendency to correct for spurious cooling more often than spurious warming; the actual warming is much less.

And a particularly cynical explanation is:

(H''') The agreement among warming estimates reflects deliberate, coordinated manipulation of the thermometer data by climate researchers in order to advance a shared environmental policy agenda; the actual warming is much less.

So now we have three alternative explanations of the agreement among warming estimates, according to which H_{1C} is false.

Each of these alternative explanations becomes much less plausible, however, in light of additional investigations that indicate a similar rise in global temperature. The Berkeley Earth project is particularly significant in this regard. It was initiated by individuals who shared contrarian concerns about the accuracy of other analyses and sought to produce an independent analysis of global temperature change. As noted earlier, they adopted a quite different approach to homogenization. The fact that they nevertheless obtained results very similar to those from HADCRUT5, GISTEMP, etc. renders much less plausible both H'' (homogenization bias) and H''' (deliberate manipulation). The Berkeley Earth group also carefully investigated several potential sources of error identified by contrarians – including those cited in H' (biased thermometer data) – but found that they made little difference to results. For example, rates of global temperature change estimated using data from better-located stations – for example, away from buildings and concrete surfaces that can be artificial heat sources – did not differ in a statistically significant way from rates estimated using data from poorly-located stations (Muller et al. 2013).

An unusual reanalysis study also helps to rule out H' (biased thermometer data). The 20th Century Reanalysis (20CR) project produced a reanalysis dataset *without using any thermometer data from land-based stations*; only surface pressure observations, monthly mean sea surface temperature data, and information about some atmospheric constituents (e.g., reflective particles from volcanic eruptions, which can have a cooling effect) were assimilated. Yet the evolution of global temperature over land according to 20CR – inferred with the help of theoretical equations relating local temperatures to other physical quantities – was *also* quite similar to that found in results produced via the standard thermometer-based methodology. (This analysis is not shown in Figure 2, which focuses on combined land/ocean temperature.) The paper announcing the result was titled, "Independent confirmation of global land warming without the use of station temperatures" (Compo et al. 2013).[7]

Schupbach (2018) adopts a Bayesian perspective to demonstrate formally the evidential value of results that discriminate among competing explanations of

---

[7] Global temperature variations estimated from independent satellite-based instruments – available for recent decades – *also* closely track thermometer-based estimates (see, e.g., Susskind et al. 2019).

other results. On a standard Bayesian view, an agent assigns to a hypothesis H a probability, $p(H)$, representing their degree of belief that H is true. Likewise, they assign probabilities to all of H's competitors, H', H'', etc., with the total probability assigned to H and its competitors summing to 1. When the agent receives new evidence, e, they update their degree of belief in each hypothesis in accordance with Bayes' Theorem: $p(H|e) = p(e|H)^*$ $p(H)/p(e)$. If this updating results in an increase in the probability assigned to H, that is, if $p(H|e) > p(H)$, then e is said to *confirm* or *support* H. Schupbach shows that a new result, $e = r_n$, which is very likely under explanatory hypothesis H but very unlikely under some of its rivals, can do just that; it will provide support for H, as probability that had previously been assigned to the now-eliminated competitors is redistributed among the remaining explanatory hypotheses, including H (see Schupbach 2018, Section 3.2 and Appendix, for details). Applying his analysis here, results from Berkeley Earth and 20CR, by ruling out competitors to H_{1C}, would increase the probability of, and thus provide some support for, H_{1C}.

Non-Bayesian philosophical theories of evidence that eschew assigning probabilities to hypotheses also would find value in the Berkeley Earth and 20CR results. For instance, on Julian Reiss's (2015) Eliminativist Hypothetico-Contextual (EHC) account, data provide *direct support* for H if they display a pattern that we are entitled to expect if H is true, and they provide *indirect support* for H if they display a pattern that is incompatible with what we are entitled to expect if rivals to H are true or if alternative (undermining) accounts of H's support – accounts that deny or cast doubt on that support – are true. From the perspective of Reiss's account, results from Berkeley Earth and 20CR provide both direct and indirect support for H_{1C}. Alternatively, adopting Deborah Mayo's (1996, 2018) error-statistical framework, the Berkeley Earth and 20CR studies can be understood as part of a broader effort to *severely test* H_{1C}, that is, to carry out a set of investigations that very probably will succeed in revealing H_{1C} to be false, just in case it is false; the Berkeley Earth and 20CR studies probe particular reasons for thinking that other temperature analyses might erroneously indicate the truth of H_{1C}.

Note that a similar evidential payoff accrues if the discussion is framed instead in terms of the adequacy-for-purpose of the HADCRUT5, GISTEMP, and NOAA data models. Consider the hypothesis that (H^*) these data models are adequate for the purpose of (P) discerning whether global temperature in 2020 was more than 1 °C warmer than during 1880–1899. There are rivals to H^* that parallel those for H_{1C}, namely, that the HADCRUT5, GISTEMP, and NOAA data models reflect similarly biased data, or similarly biased homogenization, or outright manipulation. Results from Berkeley Earth and 20CR clearly help to eliminate these possible reasons to doubt H^* too. This points to another way in which researchers can gain confidence in the adequacy-for-purpose of a data model; in addition to directly scrutinizing the details of how it was produced, that is, the assumptions of the model of the measurement process, they can obtain indirect evidence of a data model's adequacy-for-purpose when results from other investigations rule out one or more reasons for doubting or questioning its adequacy. A demonstration of robustness can sometimes do exactly that.

2.4 Good Evidence of Warming

What ultimately interests climate scientists, however, is not whether there is *some* evidence or support for the hypothesis that earth's climate is warming significantly, but whether there is *good* or *strong* evidence of this.[8] The different philosophical perspectives on evidence outlined above will cash out this idea of good or strong evidence somewhat differently. For a Bayesian, the strength of some evidence for a hypothesis H is often characterized in a comparative way, using the Bayes Factor; it equals the probability of the evidence assuming that H is true divided by its probability assuming that a rival is true. Reiss's (2015) EHC framework calls for assigning H one of several levels of warrant, ranging from weak warrant to proof, depending on the extent to which (i) H has direct support and (ii) alternative accounts of H's direct and indirect support have been eliminated. On Mayo's (1996, 2018) error-statistical account, we have good evidence for a hypothesis H if H passes a set of tests that very probably would have revealed H to be false, if (and only if) it is false. The more probable it is that the testing would have revealed H to be false, the more *severe* the testing and the stronger the evidence. Despite some deep differences, on all of these accounts, data available to climate scientists – which extend far beyond thermometer data – constitute good evidence that earth's climate has warmed significantly since the late nineteenth century.

For an illustration, let's consider H_{IC} from the perspective of the error-statistical account, which sets a demanding standard for good evidence. We need to assess whether H_{IC} is well probed – whether it has passed a set of tests that very probably would have uncovered its falsity, just in case it is false. The primary tests come via the standard and Berkeley Earth analyses. Well-motivated measurement models underlie these analyses, according to which global temperature anomalies can be estimated by aggregating local thermometer data, after correcting for known sources of error, accounting for the uneven distribution of thermometer locations, and so on. Accompanying uncertainty

---

[8] Here and below, "significant" warming means warming that makes a practical difference, not merely warming that can be detected statistically.

analyses indicate that, if actual warming between 1880–1899 and 2020 were 1°C or less, then these methods would very probably deliver estimates of warming much smaller than they actually do. (In Figure 2, the warming looks to be about 1.3°C.) H_{1C} passes these relatively probing tests with flying colors.

But this assessment takes at face value both the models of the measurement process underlying the standard and Berkeley Earth analyses and the associated uncertainty models. In practice, these models are idealized in various ways, and they omit some sources of error and uncertainty. We should consider whether these omissions and idealizations threaten the face-value findings regarding H_{1C}. For the most part, there is good reason to think that they do not.

First, consider omissions and idealizations of the measurement models underlying standard analyses. These models fail to account for some recognized (or potential) sources of systematic error in the measurement process. But the impacts of the most worrisome of these – related to heat island effects, instrument siting, and homogenization methods – have been well probed by Berkeley Earth investigations and found to not make a significant difference. Worries about thermometer data and its homogenization are further allayed by 20CR, which was produced via reanalysis and without the use of any land-based thermometer data, yet showed warming similar to thermometer-based estimates of warming over land. The impacts of some other recognized (or potential) sources of error, for example, in early ocean temperature data, and of some idealizations in the assumptions of the measurement models, stand in need of further investigation.[9] Nevertheless, even under pessimistic assumptions about their magnitude, it is implausible that their impact will be large enough to threaten H_{1C}. Moreover, remaining biases in some global temperature analyses, like that due to limited coverage of the rapidly warming Arctic, contribute to the *under*estimation of global warming (see Cowtan and Way 2014).

Second, consider omissions and idealizations of the models used to quantify uncertainties associated with global temperature anomaly estimates. These uncertainty models typically assume that the model of the measurement process employed in the study is correct; they sample and propagate uncertainties associated with measurement model inputs (e.g., thermometer readings) and parameters (e.g., in homogenization methods), but uncertainty about how to construct the measurement model in the first place (i.e., structural model uncertainty) is not addressed. Some methods have other limitations as well, for example, in how/whether they address spatiotemporal correlations in

---

[9] See, e.g., Kennedy et al. (2019). They remark: "No part of the SST [sea surface temperature] record is simple to understand or without some little mystery of its own" (p.7721).

uncertainties. Thus, some caution is needed when interpreting these uncertainty estimates. That said, it is reassuring that global temperature anomalies estimated using quite different methods (standard, reanalysis, Berkeley Earth, 20CR) usually fall within – or nearly within – the uncertainty intervals produced in other analyses; this suggests that uncertainties are not dramatically underestimated. But suppose they are dramatically underestimated. Even if the actual uncertainties are twice as large, the conclusion that there has been *significant* warming between 1880–1899 and 2020 – warming of, say, *at least 0.7°C* – would still be well warranted.[10]

Moreover, while the global temperature analyses that have been the focus of this section are important evidence that significant warming has occurred, they are far from the only evidence. Indications of a warming world can be seen throughout the climate system, in glacier retreat, sea ice loss, sea level rise, changes in animal migration, and more (IPCC 2021; see also Winsberg 2018a, Ch.2). Data documenting these changes *also* help to warrant the conclusion that earth's climate is warming significantly. We can make a qualitative severity argument: Given the breadth of climate scientists' investigations of climate system conditions, and their methodologies, they very probably would have uncovered substantial evidence challenging the warming world hypothesis if it were false, but they have not found such evidence. Instead, a wide range of findings from across the climate system converge in indicating a significantly warming world.

3 Explaining Changes in Climate

What is causing earth's climate to warm? By their Fifth Assessment Report (AR5), published in 2013, the IPCC concluded that it was *extremely likely* (probability ≥95 percent) that more than half of the increase in global temperature since 1950 was human caused (Bindoff et al. 2013, p. 869). In the IPCC's Sixth Assessment Report (AR6), appearing in 2021, human-induced warming of the climate system is deemed "unequivocal" and, for global temperature, its magnitude since the late nineteenth century is estimated to *likely* (probability ≥66 percent) be in the range 0.8–1.3°C (Eyring et al. 2021, p. 425). This is a net anthropogenic contribution, reflecting an even larger warming contribution from greenhouse gases (GHGs) – estimated to be 1.0–2.0°C – that is partially offset by cooling from anthropogenic aerosols.

This section examines how climate researchers arrive at such conclusions and highlights the important roles that computational models play in developing

---

[10] In fact, given smaller uncertainties for global temperature anomalies for more recent periods, it could be argued that global temperature has increased by at least 0.7°C even since the 1970s. See Figures 1 and 2.

quantitative explanations of climate phenomena. Section 3.1 identifies several obstacles to developing such explanations. Section 3.2 presents Ed Lorenz's (1970) vision for making progress in the face of these obstacles by using computational models as bookkeeping devices. We see this approach in action, alongside some others, in Section 3.3, which reviews how contemporary researchers investigate the causes of recent global warming. Section 3.4 discusses how the IPCC moves from the results of these investigations to conclusions about the warming contributions of GHGs and then examines one of these headline conclusions from the perspective of Julian Reiss's (2015) EHC evidential framework. Finally, Section 3.5 characterizes the explanatory progress that has been made in climate science in recent decades and identifies some explanatory pitfalls that continue to present a risk.

3.1 Obstacles to Explanation

Climate scientists seek to explain various climate phenomena, from the stability of climates over long periods, to differences in climate from region to region, to changes in climate over time, including the global warming discussed in Section 2. Typically, the explanations sought are causal. That is, the aim is to give an accurate account of how various causal factors – conditions, processes, events – together produce the climate phenomenon of interest. Yet there are several reasons why developing such explanations can be difficult.

Large causal menu. First, there are often many *potential* causal contributors to climate phenomena. In part, this is because the climate system itself is a complex system; it is composed of myriad interacting parts and processes. In addition, there are several factors considered "external" to the climate system that can influence its evolution, including but not limited to: variations in the sun's output; volcanic eruptions, which release large quantities of reflective aerosols; anthropogenic emissions of GHGs and aerosols; anthropogenic changes in properties of the land surface; and, at very long timescales, changes in earth's orbit and plate tectonics. Fluctuations in climatic conditions can occur in the absence of changes in these factors too; such "internal variability" often stems from oscillatory or chaotic phenomena in the oceans, for example, the El Niño Southern Oscillation (ENSO), the Pacific Decadal Oscillation, the Atlantic Multidecadal Oscillation, and others.[11] The task of quantitatively explaining a given climate phenomenon thus involves determining the extent to which many potential causal contributors are actual contributors.

---

[11] Their names notwithstanding, the degree to which these "oscillations" are truly oscillatory is a matter of debate.

Multiple actual causes. Oftentimes there are several actual contributors. Climate phenomena of interest often result from the joint action of multiple, partially compensating causes. Moreover, the contributions of these causal factors often are not purely additive but at least somewhat interactive and can involve feedback loops. When it comes to changes in climate, the task is rarely to identify one actual cause from a large menu of potential causes – "the" cause of a change in temperature or precipitation – but rather to understand the ways in which various external factors, as well as internal variability, have jointly resulted in the observed change.

Limited information about past causes and conditions. A further obstacle is the limited availability of information about past climate conditions and about how recognized drivers of climate change have varied in the past. Observations of temperature, precipitation, and other climate variables from ground-based instruments are available with quasi-global coverage only for the last century and a half, and satellite-based observations are available only since the late twentieth century. Key climate metrics derived from those observations, such as ocean heat content change or stratospheric temperature trends, are likewise available only for these recent periods. For earlier periods, researchers attempt to glean information about conditions from indirect indicators, such as tree rings, ice cores, and ocean sediments, but coverage and resolution are limited, and estimates of global climatic conditions derived from them often involve large uncertainties. Likewise, only so much is known about the quantity of aerosols ejected by past volcanoes, past solar variability, past emissions of GHGs and aerosols from industrial activities, and so on.

No controlled experiments. In addition, a standard scientific means of testing causal hypotheses – namely, by conducting controlled experiments – is generally unavailable in this context. A hypothesis about the effect of rising GHG concentrations on global surface temperature cannot be tested by conducting an experiment in which atmospheric concentrations of these gases are increased on one earth-like planet and kept constant on another. Not only is there just one earth, but there is no nearby planet that is even moderately similar to earth in relevant respects, which might serve as a rough analogue.

Incomplete and intractable theory. Finally, there is an obstacle related to theory. Climate science is not without theory. Simple energy-balance considerations allow for a rough calculation of an average global temperature. Many causal processes in earth's climate system – from the transport of mass and heat, to radiative transfer, to chemical reactions – are within the domains of reliable theories in fluid dynamics, physics, and chemistry. But not every causal process shaping climate is well-understood theoretically. And once researchers bring together the various relevant theoretical resources that are available, what they have is a large, complex set of equations that cannot be solved analytically. It thus can be far from straightforward to *use* available theory to develop explanations of climate phenomena.

Considering all of these factors together, we might worry that, when it comes to identifying the cause(s) of a given climate phenomenon, climate scientists will be able to formulate many hypotheses, but will be unable to tell which, if any, is correct. They might be unable to empirically test their hypotheses and, indeed, unable to even check their quantitative plausibility, given the mathematical intractability of theory. This was precisely the worry expressed by atmospheric scientist Ed Lorenz fifty years ago, in the midst of debates over the cause(s) of past ice ages. Yet he also saw a way to make progress.

3.2 Computational Models as Bookkeeping Devices

Lorenz argued that computational models could help climate scientists to test the quantitative plausibility of hypotheses about changes in climate. The approach that he envisioned involved, first, constructing a mathematical model in the form of a set of differential equations, which represented a set of causal factors (conditions, processes) that were hypothesized to bring about a given change in climate. Though the equations would be analytically unsolvable, the computer could be used to *numerically* integrate them, that is, to estimate solutions using numerical methods. One could then check whether the calculated change in conditions – a cooling of global temperature, say – was close to the observed magnitude of the change to be explained. As Lorenz explained:

> " ... one might argue convincingly that a decrease in evaporation from the ocean would bring about a decrease in surface salinity, which would inhibit vertical overturning and thereby favor the formation of sea ice, which would in turn bring about increased reflection of solar radiation, and thereby lower atmospheric temperature. Such reasoning could be completely sound, and yet not be particularly relevant to the problem of climatic change [i.e., to identifying the causes of past ice ages], if the decrease in temperature arising from a given decrease in evaporation should prove to be negligibly small, or if the decreased evaporation should simultaneously initiate a second chain of events which would favor a rise in temperature. Yet all of the essential features of this reasoning *can* be incorporated into a mathematical model, and the step-by-step numerical integration of the equations will then constitute a system of bookkeeping for the ensuing temperature changes." (Lorenz 1970, p. 327, emphasis in original)

If the hypothesis is sound, he goes on to suggest, then the model should reproduce the change in climate under investigation (Lorenz 1970, p.328). That is, the cumulative change in conditions calculated across the time steps of the computational model's integration should be similar in magnitude to the observed change.

How can these tests facilitate progress in explaining climate phenomena? If the calculated change for a given causal hypothesis fails to even roughly match the change under investigation, then scientists might reject the hypothesis, narrowing the field of candidate explanations. Care is required here, though, since a failure is not *necessarily* grounds for rejection. This is for the usual Duhemian reason: The failure might have occurred not because the hypothesis from which the prediction is derived is false, but for other reasons related to the test procedure. For instance, perhaps the numerical methods used to integrate the equations did not deliver accurate enough solutions. Or perhaps the equations inadequately represented some of the important causal factors and processes hypothesized to bring about the change. But to the extent that scientists have good reason to think that such alternative reasons for a model's failure to reproduce an observed change in climate are unlikely, they have grounds for doubting the causal hypothesis under test. By contrast, if a simulation model does reproduce the observed change, this suggests that the causal hypothesis under test is quantitatively plausible and remains a candidate explanation of the change. It clearly does not on its own establish that the hypothesis correctly identifies the actual cause(s) of the observed change, since there might be other plausible ways to account for that change.

Looking forward to the twenty-first century, Lorenz imagined a "super-model" of the climate system, intended to represent not just the causal factors relevant to learning the implications of a particular hypothesis, but all of the causal factors that might conceivably have influenced past changes in climate. Experimenting on such a model – changing the distribution of ice sheets or adjusting the composition of the atmosphere – might reveal additional plausible hypotheses about the causes of a past climatic change. As Lorenz puts it: "In essence, we will have reached the day when mathematical procedures will be instrumental in formulating hypotheses as well as testing them" (1970, p. 329). But he also emphasizes: "As to what features *did* produce climatic changes, we shall still have the privilege of arguing" (Lorenz 1970, emphasis in original).

3.3 Investigating the Causes of Recent Warming

Fifty years later, computational models of the climate system still fall short of the super-models that Lorenz imagined, but they have developed substantially in that direction. Successive generations of climate models have grown more and more comprehensive in their representation of causal processes in the climate system. They *are* used to test the quantitative plausibility of causal hypotheses in the way envisioned by Lorenz and, more generally, to simulate how changes in different causal factors would, in various combinations, impact climate conditions. They also sometimes serve as resources for formulating and refining hypotheses about the causes of climate phenomena.

The most comprehensive and detailed of these climate models are known as *general circulation models* (GCMs) or *earth system models* (ESMs). They consist of a set of interacting sub-models, each representing processes in one part of the climate system – atmosphere, ocean, land surface, ice sheets, and so on. Each sub-model represents conditions on a set of grid points, where each point is associated with a volume of atmosphere, or ocean, or land surface, etc. For simulations to be computationally tractable, these grid points need to be relatively widely spaced, for example, on the order of 100 km in the horizontal for the atmosphere. For each grid point, a set of equations is specified, meant to describe how average conditions in the associated volume (grid box) will change over a short time period – minutes to hours – in response to causal processes operating in the grid box and those adjacent to it. For the atmosphere, these equations include a discretized set of core equations from fluid dynamics and thermodynamics ("the dynamical core") whose state variables include temperature, pressure, and wind speed in the north–south, east–west and verti-cal directions, as well as many additional equations ("the physics") intended to capture the effects of other physical processes that can influence the state variables, such as radiation transfer and the formation of clouds and precipita-tion. Although many of these physical processes operate at scales smaller than the model's grid-scale, they must be represented as a function of grid-scale variables; this practice is known as *parameterization*.[12] To simulate the evolu-tion of conditions over a decade or century or longer, the modeling equations for each grid point are solved repeatedly using numerical methods, in effect stepping conditions forward a short time, then stepping them forward again, and so on. Statistical properties of the simulated conditions can then be calcu-lated to estimate the values of climate variables, such as the average and range of temperature in a region over several decades.

The use of these models in a bookkeeping role, as envisioned by Lorenz, is readily illustrated in research investigating the causes of recent global warming. To test the quantitative plausibility of the hypothesis that (H_{NAT}) *increases in global temperature since the late nineteenth century were caused mainly by natural factors*, in particular changes in solar output, volcanic activity, and internal variability, researchers run simulations in which anthropogenic factors

---

[12] Typically, there is not an obviously best way to parameterize a given process and different modeling groups take somewhat different approaches. See also Section 4.1.

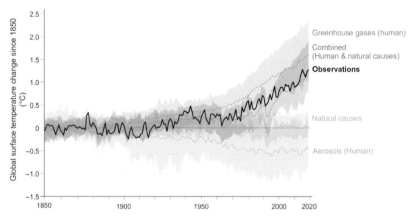

Figure 3 Global temperature change in observations compared to climate model simulations. Shading indicates the 5–95 percent range of results across the simulations. (Source: FAQ 3.1, Figure 1 in IPCC 2021: Chapter 3. Reprinted with permission.)

are held fixed at preindustrial levels, while these natural factors are allowed to vary in accordance with historical estimates (see "Natural causes" in Figure 3). Since these simulations do not come remotely close to reproducing observed warming, H_{NAT} appears quantitatively implausible (see also Odenbaugh 2018). By contrast, when anthropogenic factors, including GHGs and aerosols, are also allowed to vary in accordance with historical estimates, the resulting simulations *are* found to roughly track variations in global temperature (see "Combined" in Figure 3).[13] In conjunction with the findings regarding H_{NAT}, this indicates the quantitative plausibility of the hypothesis that (H_{ANTH}) *increases in global temperature since the late nineteenth century were caused mainly by anthropogenic factors*. A further finding is that, when *only* GHG concentrations are allowed to vary in accordance with historical estimates, and natural and other anthropogenic factors are held fixed at preindustrial levels, simulations show warming that somewhat *exceeds* that which is observed, consistent with the idea that GHG-induced warming is being partially offset by the cooling effect of reflective anthropogenic aerosols (see "Greenhouse gases (human)" and "Aerosols (human)" in Figure 3).

---

[13] The same is also true for a number of other climate variables: Simulations with natural factors alone do not come close to accounting for the observed changes in these variables, but simulations with combined natural and anthropogenic factors (roughly) do. See illustrations at NASA's Scientific Visualization Studio: https://svs.gsfc.nasa.gov/4908/.

GCMs/ESMs also play important roles in more sophisticated investigations of the causes of recent warming.[14] In *attribution* studies, one or more climate models are used to estimate the *spatiotemporal pattern* of change in a climate variable that would emerge if a given causal factor (or set of factors) varied in accordance with historical estimates, while others were held fixed. For each factor, this pattern will show more change in some locations and time periods than others. Insofar as the patterns for different causal factors are distinct, they serve as *fingerprints* of those causal factors. Researchers then find the (weighted) linear combination of fingerprints that best fits the observations and check whether the residual change can plausibly be ascribed to internal variability, that is, to variation that occurs even in the absence of any forcing of the climate system. If so, and if the weights assigned to the fingerprints are close to 1, this indicates the quantitative plausibility of the hypothesis that the observed change was caused by the specified factors.[15]

Estimates of the contributions of different causal factors can then be inferred from these weights.[16] These estimates are subject to significant uncertainty, however, stemming from: uncertainty about the fingerprint patterns themselves, due to climate model limitations; similarity between the patterns estimated for different factors, that is, degeneracy; and the fact that the observed patterns of change to be accounted for also have some associated uncertainty. The upshot is that conclusions about the contributions of different causal factors cannot be very precise. For example, drawing primarily on attribution (i.e., fingerprint) studies, the IPCC concluded in AR5 that "greenhouse gases contributed a global mean surface warming *likely* to be in the range of 0.5°C to 1.3°C over the period 1951 to 2010" (IPCC 2013, p. 17). We will examine the basis for such conclusions in more detail in Section 3.4.

In addition to studies involving climate models, there are empirical investigations of the causes of recent warming, which employ methods from statistics and econometrics. A study by Folland et al. (2018) provides a nice illustration. They showed that the monthly global temperature record for the period 1891–2015 could be reconstructed using equations produced via cross-validation multiple regression, taking historical variations in known natural and anthropogenic forcing factors and modes of internal variability as the independently estimated predictors and the

---

[14] What follows is a very simplified description of attribution studies, intended to convey their most basic elements. For technical details, consult Bindoff et al. (2013) and references therein.

[15] There are several reasons why the estimated weights might deviate from 1, even if the hypothesis under investigation is correct. Most obviously, the model-estimated fingerprints might contain significant errors. To the extent that the estimated weights *are* close to 1, this provides some reassurance both that the causal factors have been correctly identified and that the models are simulating the contributions of those factors reasonably well (see Parker 2010).

[16] Both model-based and empirical attribution methods typically assume that contributions from different causal factors are additive, i.e., do not exhibit interactive effects. This is thought to be a reasonable approximation for global temperature but not in some other cases.

1891–2015 time series of monthly global temperature anomalies as the predictand. An example of such an equation is:

$$GST = -0.0595 + 0.0172*AMO + 0.0617*ENSO + 0.0441*VOLC$$
$$+ 0.0457*TSI + 0.2802*GA + 0.0219*AO$$

here, GST represents the global temperature for a given month, the other variables (AMO, ENSO, VOLC, TSI, GA, and AO) represent the normalized magnitudes of different causal factors in that month, and the coefficient on each variable represents that factor's global warming or cooling potency as estimated via regression. Since the historical magnitudes of the forcing factors and of GST are somewhat uncertain, Folland et al. generated many such regression equations, sampling these uncertainties, and took the average of these as the best-estimate regression equation. The time series of GST reconstructed with that best-estimate equation showed good fit to observations. They concluded: " . . . the generally high reconstruction accuracy shows that known external and internal forcing factors explain all the main variations in [global temperature] between 1891 and 2015, allowing for our current understanding of their uncertainties. Accordingly, no important additional factors are needed to explain the two main warming and three main slowdown periods [i.e., the main variations in global temperature] during this epoch" (Folland et al. 2018, eaao5297).

Importantly, Folland et al.'s reconstruction achieved a good fit not just for periods of rapid global warming, but also for periods in which little or no global warming occurred. In fact, these slowdown periods (1896–1910, 1941–1975, and 1998–2013) were the main focus of the study. Prima facie, they present a puzzle: If GHG concentrations continued to rise rapidly, why didn't global temperature? Indeed, the occurrence of the most recent slowdown (or "hiatus") from roughly 1998–2013, and the fact that many climate models projected greater warming for the period, was claimed by climate contrarians to show that GHGs are not the primary cause of recent global warming after all. Thus, in addition to regression equations generated using the full 1891–2015 time series, for each slowdown period Folland et al. produced regression equations leaving out that slowdown period. They then used the equations that were produced leaving out the slowdown period to predict what conditions in the slowdown period would be, again generally with good success. Folland et al.'s analysis indicates that, during these slowdown periods, less warming *is what we should expect to find*, given the causal factors that operated during those periods. On their analysis, during the most recent "hiatus," anthropogenic warming continued unabated, but a substantial portion of it was offset by cooling contributions from internal variability (ENSO/IPO), reduced solar irradiance (TSI), and increased volcanic activity (VOLC) (see Folland et al. 2018, Figure 6D).

Other research investigating the recent "hiatus" employed climate models in the bookkeeping roles described earlier. For example, one hypothesis was that a particular mode of internal variability (namely, La Niña-like conditions in the tropical Pacific Ocean) was a significant contributor to the slowdown in warming. Huber and Knutti (2014) investigated the expected contribution of this factor by identifying "variability analogues" – fifteen-year segments of unforced climate simulations in which the pattern of tropical Pacific variability resembled that observed during the hiatus; they found that global temperatures tended to cool by $0.06 \pm 0.12°C$/decade in these segments (see also Stolpe et al. 2017). This is similar in magnitude to the cooling contribution later estimated empirically (for ENSO/IPO) by Folland et al. (2018, Figure 6C) with smaller uncertainty bounds.[17] The Pacific variability hypothesis had gained attention a few years earlier in light of another model-based study: When Meehl et al. (2011) examined segments of climate simulations in which GHG concentrations were increasing but global temperature nevertheless exhibited warming slowdowns, they noticed that, in these slowdown periods, a La Niña-like pattern of variability tended to prevail, with more heat than usual being transported into the deeper layers of the oceans. As they put it: "The model provides a plausible depiction of processes in the climate system causing the hiatus periods, and indicates that a hiatus period is a relatively common climate phenomenon and may be linked to La Niña-like conditions" (Meehl et al. 2011, p. 360). Here, simulations played a role akin to that which Lorenz envisioned for a super-model of the climate system – they aided hypothesis *formulation*.

In the end, employing results from a wide range of studies, researchers were able to demonstrate that a slowdown in warming during the recent hiatus period was to be expected, given the causal factors understood to be present over the period.[18] Moreover, the greater warming that had been projected by many climate models did not indicate a deep problem with the science as climate contrarians claimed; indeed, the mismatch was readily accounted for. First, most of the model projections – as expected – were not in phase with Pacific internal variability over the period, which is akin to noise; those simulations that did happen to track Pacific variability also showed less warming (Risbey et al. 2014). Second, while

---

[17] While these magnitudes seem small, they constitute a substantial fraction of slowdown in warming that was to be explained.

[18] Interestingly, the extent of the slowdown itself was also found to be exaggerated in some observational datasets, due to coverage bias (see Cowtan and Way 2014). If warming of the Arctic is accelerating, datasets that do not fill in gaps in the Arctic (e.g., by spatial interpolation) will increasingly underestimate global temperature change.

the forward-looking projections had made reasonable assumptions about what solar irradiance, volcanic activity and anthropogenic emissions would be like over the period, these turned out to differ somewhat from what subsequently actually occurred. Taking account of the actual pattern of internal variability over the period and estimates of actual volcanic activity, emissions, and so on, the mismatch between models and observations largely disappears (see Huber and Knutti 2014; Schmidt et al. 2014).

3.4 Reaching Causal Conclusions

In light of these and other studies investigating the causes of recent global warming, IPCC scientists have arrived at conclusions like the following:

MOST: It is *extremely likely* that more than half of the global warming observed since 1950 was anthropogenic (IPCC 2013).

QUANT: It is *likely* that well-mixed GHGs contributed a warming of 1.0–2.0°C since the late nineteenth century (Eyring et al. 2021).

This section will discuss how the IPCC arrives at conclusions like MOST and QUANT and will show that the headline conclusion MOST accords well with an evaluation from the perspective of Julian Reiss's (2015) EHC evidence framework.

The IPCC Approach to Evidence Assessment

The IPCC is currently divided into three Working Groups, which focus on different aspects of the climate change issue. Working Group 1 (WG1) focuses on the physical science basis, Working Group 2 focuses on climate change impacts and adaptation, and Working Group 3 focuses on mitigation strategies. Within each Working Group are chapter teams that address particular topics. Each chapter team is tasked with examining and synthesizing published research on their assigned topic, considering how that research bears on key questions, and reporting conclusions that reflect the consensus of the chapter team. Human influence on the climate system was the topic of Chapter 10 of the WG1 contribution to AR5 (IPCC 2013) and Chapter 3 of the WG1 contribution to AR6 (IPCC 2021).

In developing their conclusions, IPCC chapter teams are asked to consider both the nature of the evidence that is available – its type, amount, quality, and consistency – and the extent to which that evidence is in agreement in supporting particular conclusions (Mastrandrea et al. 2011). Available evidence can be assessed as *limited*, *medium*, or *robust*, while agreement can be characterized as *low*, *medium*, or *high*. In light of this evaluation, chapter teams can report a qualitative level of confidence in a finding or conclusion: *low*, *medium*, *high*, or *very high* confidence. If they judge that more can be said – in particular, that a probability can be assessed – then they can report that as well. The IPCC provides calibrated language for reporting these probabilities (see Table 1). Thus, when the IPCC chapter team reports in AR6 that it is "likely" that well-mixed GHGs contributed a warming of 1.0–2.0°C, this indicates that they assessed there to be *a probability of at least 66 percent* that the warming contribution was in that range.

The IPCC approach to evidence assessment, including its confidence and likelihood terminology, has been praised by some commentators, but it has also been the target of criticism. Critics have argued that it is unclear how its likelihoods/probabilities should be interpreted, that its application by author teams leads to incoherent shifts between frequentist and subjective probabilities, and more. Some criticisms have been leveled by scientists, while others have come from philosophers of science, in some cases with suggestions for improvement or proposals for coherent interpretation (recent contributions include, e.g., Rehg and Staley 2017; Harris 2021; Dethier 2023a; see also Adler and Hirsch Hadorn 2014). Issues related to the IPCC's use of these likelihoods – and other concerns with the IPCC's approach to evidence assessment – will be bracketed here, though they are worthy of attention and discussion. The aim here is simply to introduce the IPCC approach to evidence evaluation and to illustrate its application. Ultimately, the approach is a practice-based attempt at solving a very difficult problem: Trying to ensure that dozens of chapter teams, tackling widely different topics, assess large bodies of evidence in a reasonable way and communicate differential evidential support for conclusions in a manner that is consistent across different parts of the report and is understandable for its readers.

Table 1 Calibrated likelihood language adopted by the IPCC. See Mastrandrea et al. (2011).

Term	Probability range
Virtually certain	99–100%
Extremely likely	95–100%
Very likely	90–100%
Likely	66–100%
More likely than not	>50–100%
About as likely as not	33–66%
Unlikely	0–33%
Very unlikely	0–10%
Extremely unlikely	0–5%
Exceptionally unlikely	0–1%

Reaching Conclusions about Human Influence

IPCC chapters typically provide a summary of relevant evidence and findings from previous assessments and then focus their discussion on new studies produced since the last assessment. Figure 4 summarizes new evidence considered in AR6 when assessing the contributions of different causal factors to global warming since the late nineteenth century. Here, the primary evidence consists of results from three attribution studies, two of which employed multi-model average fingerprints (Gillett et al. 2021; Ribes et al. 2021) and one of which took a more empirical approach (Haustein et al. 2017). Results produced using an alternative radiative-forcing-based approach, discussed in Chapter 7 of the same IPCC report, are also shown. Likewise, results from thirteen GCMs/ESMs are shown, to give a sense of the range of contributions indicated by individual models. (Results from

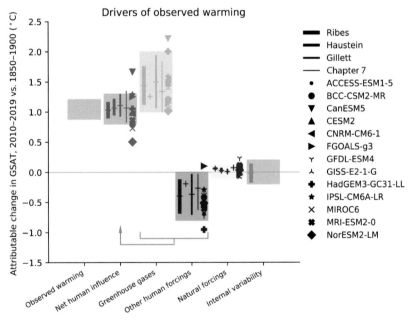

Figure 4 Assessed contributions to observed warming and underlying evidence. Plain shaded band shows the estimated 5–95 percent range of observed warming. Other shaded bands show IPCC expert assessed *likely* ranges of temperature change in global surface air temperature (GSAT), 2010–2019 relative to 1850–1900, attributable to different causal factors. Vertical bars show 5–95 percent uncertainty ranges produced in four different analyses, with their best estimates of contributions represented by crosses (+). Other symbols show the simulated responses from each of the climate models indicated. (Source: Figure 3.8 in IPCC 2021: Chapter 3. Reprinted with permission.)

such GCMs/ESMs are combined to determine the multi-model average finger-prints used in the two model-based attribution studies.)

Whether the available evidence regarding human influence on global tempera-ture should be considered *limited*, *medium*, or *robust* is not stated in AR6, but similar evidence from earlier studies was already deemed *robust* in AR5.[19] The AR6 chapter team did note the *agreement* among the primary lines of evidence shown in Figure 4: "In spite of their different methodologies and input datasets, the three attribution approaches yield very similar results, with the anthropogenic attributable warming range encompassing observed warming, and the natural attributable warming being close to zero" (Eyring et al. 2021, p. 440). They further note: "Estimates based on physical understanding of forcing and ECS [Equilibrium Climate Sensitivity] made by Chapter 7 are close to estimates from attribution studies, despite being the products of a different approach. This agreement enhances confidence in the magnitude and causes of attributable surface temperature warming" (Eyring et al. 2021, pp. 440–441).

Though these lines of evidence are in good agreement, it is not obvious how they should be combined to reach *overall* conclusions about the contributions of differ-ent causal factors. Here, the IPCC took a simple and conservative approach. They derived "assessed" contributions for different causal factors – shown by the wide shaded bars in Figure 4 – by finding the smallest range (with a precision of $0.1\,^\circ C$) that spanned all three of the attribution studies' 5–95 percent uncertainty ranges for a given factor. For greenhouse gases, for example, this range is 1.0–$2.0\,^\circ C$. These covering ranges, which are broader than each of the 5–95 percent uncertainty ranges estimated in the individual studies, are then assessed by the IPCC to be only *likely* (i.e., probability ≥ 66 percent) to include the actual contribution, given sources of uncertainty not adequately accounted for in the individual studies. This downgrading of likelihood – from what might have been taken to be a *very likely* (probability ≥ 90 percent) range to only a *likely* range – also constitutes an informal means of taking account of results from other studies, like the Chapter 7 estimates, as well as earlier studies.[20] In this way, the IPCC arrived at conclusions like QUANT.

---

[19] The chapter on attribution in AR5 included a table that concisely presented both the evidence underlying each key conclusion as well as the chapter team's assessment of that evidence in terms of the recommended IPCC approach (i.e., evidence is *limited*, *medium*, or *robust* and exhibits *low*, *medium*, or *high* agreement). AR6 did not include such a table. Such information tends to be omitted when evidence is considered clearly sufficient to reach confident conclusions, perhaps to avoid making reports *even longer*; the WG1 contribution to AR6 exceeded 2,400 densely written pages!

[20] Why the Chapter 7 results did not factor directly into the determination of the assessed ranges is unclear. Regardless, Figure 4 makes plain that including the Chapter 7 estimates when deriving covering ranges would make almost no difference to the findings.

A very similar process of analysis had taken place in AR5. Assessed contributions for different causal factors were obtained via covering ranges derived from the 5–95 percent ranges from two attribution studies employing multi-model fingerprints, and then these covering ranges were deemed *likely* (see Bindoff et al. 2013). As was later the case in AR6 (see Figure 4), the anthropogenic warming contribution in AR5 was found to be *similar in magnitude to the observed warming*, though in AR5 the period of analysis was shorter, from 1950 onwards. The headline AR5 conclusion MOST was justified as follows: "Both optimal detection [i.e., fingerprint studies] and time series studies agree in robust detection of anthropogenic influence that is substantially more than half of the observed warming" (Bindoff et al. 2013, Table 10.1). Outside of the IPCC process, NASA climate scientist Gavin Schmidt showed that, if the IPCC's assessed *likely* range is assumed to constitute the middle 66 percent of a Normal uncertainty distribution, then the probability that anthropogenic factors were responsible for less than half of the observed warming is <0.02 percent (Schmidt 2013). Using the IPCC's calibrated terminology, it might have been deemed *virtually certain*, not just *extremely likely*, that human activities are responsible for more than half the warming.

There are several noteworthy features of the IPCC's process of arriving at conclusions about the contributions of different causal factors to recent warming. First, no attempt is made to formally aggregate the many individual pieces of evidence that are available; these include not just the latest attribution results, such as those shown in Figure 4, but also results available in previous assessment cycles as well. Such an aggregation would be very difficult to perform, in part because of complex interdependencies among the data and models used in the studies. Instead, insofar as the latest results are broadly consistent with previous ones, a simple, pragmatic approach that focuses on the latest results is taken. Second, the analysis prioritizes estimates obtained using multi-model average fingerprints, rather than estimates obtained from individual models. Multi-model averages often outperform individual models when simulations of past climate are compared to observations; averaging can help to wash out some of the errors of individual models.[21] Third, there is a downgrading of likelihood in order to account for remaining sources of uncertainty; the covering 5–95 percent uncertainty ranges are considered only *likely*. All three of the features just identified – lack of formal aggregation of evidence, a focus on findings undergirded by results from multiple climate models, and downgrading by one

---

[21] There are, however, theoretical concerns that the average fingerprint (and, more generally, the average of a set of results from different models) might not be physically consistent, i.e., consistent with underlying physical laws.

likelihood category to account for remaining uncertainties – are common in the context of IPCC assessments, not just when the focus is on attribution.

Applying Philosophical Theories of Evidence

The IPCC approach to evidence evaluation is not built upon any particular theory of evidence; as suggested earlier, it is a practice-based approach meant to facilitate a specific scientific assessment process. Nevertheless, if we attempt to relate the IPCC approach to existing theories, it is perhaps best characterized as an informal and imprecise Bayesian approach. There is often an updating of a prior level of confidence in (or probability of) a given conclusion – as reported in the previous IPCC assessment report – in light of new findings, though this is not done via an explicit calculation using Bayes' Theorem. The approach is imprecise in that it employs qualitative levels of confidence (e.g., *very high*, *high*, *medium*, *low*, etc.) and/or imprecise probability ranges (as shown in Table 1) rather than precise probabilities. Some researchers have in fact characterized related inference practices in climate science as "informal Bayesian" ones (see Schmidt and Sherwood 2015; Sherwood et al. 2020).

A different theory of evidence that is readily applicable here is Julian Reiss's (2015) Eliminativist Hypothetico-Contextualist (EHC) account, introduced briefly in Section 2. On this account, data provide *direct support* for H if they display a pattern that we are entitled to expect if H is true, and they provide *indirect support* for H if they display a pattern that is incompatible with what we are entitled to expect if rivals to H are true or if alternative (undermining) accounts of H's support – accounts that deny or cast doubt on that support – are true (Reiss 2015, p.348). As shown in Table 2, grades of overall *warrant* for H are then determined by the extent to which H has direct support as well as

Table 2 Reiss's Grades of Warrant. A *relevant* alternative is, roughly, one deemed a genuine possibility in the context at hand. A *salient* alternative is one that has some direct support. After Reiss (2015, Table 1).

Grade	Name	Requires direct support for H plus indirect support that …
1	*Proof*	eliminates all relevant alternative accounts
2	*Strong warrant*	eliminates all salient alternative accounts and some that are nonsalient
3	*Moderate warrant*	eliminates most alternatives, including some that are salient
4	*Weak warrant*	eliminates some alternative accounts

indirect support that eliminates relevant alternatives, where these alternatives can be rivals to H or alternative (undermining) accounts of H's support (e.g., that the method used to produce data supporting H was biased). Depending on the extent to which such alternatives are eliminated, hypotheses are assigned a grade of *weak warrant, moderate warrant, strong warrant,* or *proof.*

Let's consider, from the perspective of Reiss's account, the hypothesis embedded in MOST, that is, (H_{MOST}) *more than half of the global warming observed since 1950 was anthropogenic.* Direct support for H_{MOST} is found in global temperature data that display patterns that fit reasonably well with the predictions of both simulations and regression-based equations in which anthropogenic warming is dominant (as discussed in Section 3.3).[22] Gridded temperature datasets also exhibit spatiotemporal patterns that are expected if anthropogenic warming is dominant, as revealed in fingerprint studies. The same patterns in data provide indirect support for H_{MOST} as well, insofar as they are incompatible with what is expected due to changes in solar irradiance, internal variability, and so on. As the IPCC put it in AR5: "There is strong evidence that excludes solar forcing, volcanoes and internal variability as the strongest drivers of warming since 1950" (Bindoff et al. 2013, p. 871). For at least a decade now, the consensus position within climate science has been that all rivals to H_{MOST} – hypotheses attributing the majority of recent warming to causal factors other than increasing greenhouse gas concentrations – have been eliminated. Doubts about this support for H_{MOST}, stemming from the fact that climate models and attribution methodologies involve various simplifications and idealizations, are to a significant extent allayed by the fact that findings are robust to a range of changes in models, methodologies, and statistical assumptions (see Bindoff et al. 2013; Eyring et al. 2021; also Parker 2010 and Lloyd 2015). In Reiss's terminology, then, the level of warrant for H_{MOST} appears to be that of at least *strong warrant* and perhaps even (fallible and empirical) *proof.* This accords well with the IPCC's assessment that H_{MOST} is *extremely likely*, that is, has ≥ 95 percent probability of being correct.

Yet not everyone agrees that H_{MOST} is so well warranted. Dissenters include not only climate contrarians but also some scientists and philosophers who are unconvinced that all relevant alternatives have been eliminated. For instance, some contend that recent warming could be caused by variations in the level of galactic cosmic rays reaching earth, which are modulated by solar activity and can

---

[22] Projections of global temperature from earlier generations of climate models have also been found to track observed changes reasonably well – these are out-of-sample tests of their predictions – though the comparison is complicated by the fact that actual forcings over a projection period always differ somewhat from those assumed when making the projections (see, e.g., Hausfather 2017).

affect cloud formation. Climate models do not standardly take account of variations in galactic cosmic rays, nor of the mechanisms by which they might affect cloud formation, so the evidence cited earlier from modeling studies does not speak directly to this alternative hypothesis. Nevertheless, laboratory and observational studies appear to eliminate it, and the IPCC reports with *high confidence* that the contribution of cosmic rays to warming over the period 1750–2019 is "negligible" (Forster et al. 2021, p. 958).

This sort of challenge regarding the evidence for H_{MOST} has also been leveled by philosopher Joel Katzav (2013). He argues that climate researchers have not convincingly ruled out some alternatives to H_{MOST} according to which GHGs are responsible for somewhat less than half of the observed warming, with internal variability and other factors making a larger contribution than is usually claimed. This concern is underwritten in part by the fact that attribution studies tend to rely on simulation-based best-guess estimates of internal variability; a more thorough investigation of the plausible magnitude of internal variability is required, he argues, before H_{MOST} will be well warranted. Katzav's analysis here employs Mayo's (1996, 2018) error-statistical account, discussed in Section 2. His position is essentially that, from the perspective of Mayo's account, there is not yet good evidence for H_{MOST}, because H_{MOST} is not sufficiently well probed; not enough has been done to rule out some alternatives to it. He does concede, however, that there might be good evidence for the weaker hypothesis that *some* of the post-1950 warming is anthropogenic; this is a conclusion that was deemed *virtually certain* in AR5 (Bindoff et al. 2013) and "unequivocal" in AR6 (Eyring et al. 2021, p. 506).

Perhaps research conducted more recently, including that discussed in Section 3.3, is enough to convince some earlier critics that there is now at least *strong warrant* (in Reiss's sense) for H_{MOST}. If not, are holdouts simply unreasonable or not arguing in good faith? Not necessarily, according to Reiss. His theory is a pragmatist one. He contends that the decision to reject an alternative hypothesis involves a judgment that the evidence is sufficient and that, for various contextual reasons, including differences in value commitments, parties might reasonably disagree in their judgments. Differences in value commitments, for instance, might underwrite different judgments of how bad it would be to erroneously reject an alternative hypothesis, and thus lead to different views on when evidence is sufficient. As he puts it: "Support and logic by themselves do not compel a decision one way or another" (2015, p. 354).

Holdouts might also think it likely that there are causal factors contributing significantly to recent warming that simply haven't been identified yet, given the complexity of the climate system. But while it is not unreasonable to think that some small contributors have not yet been identified, for it to turn out that most warming since the late nineteenth century is due to some currently unrecognized factor, with greenhouse gases playing only a small role, a wealth of existing evidence regarding how GHGs and other factors affect global temperature, including not only results from climate models but also evidence drawn from empirical analyses like Folland et al. (2018) and from analyses of paleoclimatic data, would all have to turn out to be significantly misleading. These varied lines of evidence indicate a best estimate for GHG warming that is not merely half of observed warming but *larger than observed warming*, as illustrated in Figures 3 and 4; H_{MOST} is already a conservative conclusion. It is worth noting, too, that great deal of effort has been made, not just by climate scientists but by climate contrarians as well, to identify other causal factors that are plausibly responsible for the bulk of recent warming, with little success. Given this, one might think that H_{MOST} obtains some support via what Richard Dawid and coauthors (2015) call "nonempirical confirmation" or the "no-alternatives argument": Despite a sustained and genuine effort to find a viable alternative to H_{MOST} according to which the majority of recent warming is due to some factor other than GHGs, none has been found, though many have been proposed.

Finally, it is worth remembering that IPCC headline conclusions about anthropogenic contributions to recent warming, like headline conclusions about the occurrence of the warming itself (see Section 2), are undergirded by a broad set of findings that go beyond observed changes in near-surface temperatures. As the IPCC puts it: "Large-scale indicators of climate change in the atmosphere, ocean, cryosphere and at the land surface show clear responses to human influence consistent with those expected based on model simulations and physical understanding" (Eyring et al. 2021, p. 425; see also Fn.13 above). In other words, there is direct support in Reiss's sense for substantial human influence on climate not just in what is observed regarding surface temperature change, but also in observed patterns of change in many other climate system properties. It is in light of this totality of evidence that the IPCC now attaches no probabilistic qualifier to the conclusion that human influence has warmed the climate system to some extent since preindustrial times; that such influence has occurred is deemed "an established fact" (Arias et al. 2021, p. 41).

3.5 Progress and Pitfalls in Explanation

Over the last fifty years, explanatory practice in climate science has moved well beyond qualitative speculation about the causes of climate phenomena.

Using climate models as bookkeeping devices, and employing empirical analysis methods too, it is now possible for climate researchers to test the quantitative plausibility of various causal hypotheses and, more generally, to estimate quantitatively the contributions of different causal factors to a given climate phenomenon. As we have seen when it comes to explaining recent global warming, climate scientists can do more than just point to an enhanced greenhouse effect as a qualitative global warming mechanism; they can estimate *how much* the greenhouse effect has been enhanced by increased concentrations of carbon dioxide and other GHGs and *how much* various other factors have contributed to recent warming. And they can do so in more than a back-of-the-envelope way; their analyses attend to the spatiotemporal patterns of change that result from complex causal interactions in the climate system.

At the same time, quantitative explanations in climate science remain strikingly imprecise. The IPCC considers it extremely likely that *at least half* of post-1950 warming – not that, say, 89 percent of it – is anthropogenic. Very precise claims are precluded by the various obstacles to explanation presented in Section 3.1. Researchers only have so much information about the temperature fluctuations, methane emissions, solar variations, volcanic emissions, and so on of the past. And state-of-the-art climate models give somewhat different estimates of the response of the climate system to such drivers, owing to differences in the way the models represent various climate system processes; these differences in representation are a consequence of both incomplete theory and limited computer power. The upshot is that quantitative estimates of causal contributions to climate phenomena often have significant uncertainties, and so confident conclusions about those contributions must remain imprecise.

The obstacles to explanation identified in Section 3.1 also increase the risk of some serious explanatory pitfalls. One pitfall consists in *explaining away* challenges to existing understanding. Given a large causal menu of potential explainers, as well as significant uncertainties associated with the contributions of these different causal factors, a wide range of phenomena can be given post-hoc explanations that are at least roughly consistent with existing understanding. Phenomenon X might be explained with the help of one subset of modeling results and relatively extreme but not wholly implausible assumptions about the past intensity of particular forcings; but if not-X had occurred instead, then it might have been similarly possible to account for it in terms of a different subset of modeling results and still somewhat plausible assumptions about forcings. The worry is that, if genuine challenges to existing understanding arise – akin to Kuhnian anomalies – they will be explained away, rather than recognized as such. The risk of explaining away seems exacerbated by the fact that climate change is such a politically charged subject. When climate contrarians insist that phenomenon X undermines key conclusions about climate change, there is pressure on climate scientists to show that, in fact, it is possible to account for X without any substantive revision to existing understanding.

A closely related pitfall is a *hasty explanation*. Here the problem is too quickly assuming that a quantitatively plausible explanation of a phenomenon is the actual explanation. Arguably, this pitfall occurred in research into the recent "hiatus." Some researchers saw Pacific internal variability and changes in external forcing as competing explanations of the hiatus. One high-profile simulation study found that, if surface temperatures in a small part of the modeled Pacific Ocean were required to match those observed during the hiatus period, then global temperatures in the simulations tracked observations in an impressive way (see Kosaka and Xie 2013). The study's conclusion was that Pacific variability was therefore the actual cause of the hiatus – a conclusion that other researchers promptly called out as too hasty. Moderate confidence that the hiatus resulted from a combination of Pacific variability and changes in external forcing, with each playing a substantial but difficult-to-precisely-quantify role, emerged gradually in light of a large body of research, both model-based and empirical.

The hiatus episode thus illustrates another noteworthy feature of explanatory practice in contemporary climate science: Very often, explanations are developed in a gradual and piecemeal way, drawing on results from multiple models and other methods of analysis as well. By contrast, general philosophical discussions of models and explanations often seem to assume that explanations are to be constructed using, or even delivered by, a single model – often a relatively simple mathematical model. A central puzzle is then how such a model can explain despite incorporating idealizations, fictions, and so on (for a survey of views, see Jebeile and Kennedy 2015 or Bokulich 2017). Explanatory practice in climate science illustrates that, at least in some sciences, what occurs is not this simple form of *model explanation*, but rather a more complex and messy process of *explaining with the help of models*. When it comes to explanatory practice in these sciences, the question of how "false" models can provide explanatory information remains, but it is just one important question alongside a number of others – about how results from various studies are synthesized, used to rule out alternative explanations, used to bound uncertainties, and so on. These other questions merit more attention from philosophers of science.

4 Projecting Future Climate Change

What will climate be like in the future? This question is particularly challenging to answer. In part, this because which climate conditions will materialize in the future depends on human choices made between now and then, which will determine whether anthropogenic GHG emissions continue to rise rapidly or are substantially curbed. This obstacle to prediction is partly overcome in practice by making predictions conditional on assumptions about future atmospheric GHG concentrations; these conditional predictions are known as *projections*.

Yet even projections have substantial uncertainty. This might seem unsurprising, given that the weather typically cannot be forecasted accurately much beyond a week. But weather and climate prediction differ in a crucial respect: While weather prediction seeks to predict the atmosphere's future trajectory based on conditions today – it seeks to predict the order in which weather conditions will unfold – climate prediction aims to predict the *statistical distribution* of weather conditions that would occur in a locale when considered over a long time period, such as several decades (see Smith 2002). The chaotic nature of the atmosphere entails that trajectories can be hard to predict beyond the near future, because small errors in initial conditions can grow rapidly over time, but chaos is not necessarily a problem for climate prediction. In many cases, projections of future climate conditions are uncertain primarily because of modeling uncertainty, that is, uncertainty about how to adequately model, within the constraints of available computing power, the many causal processes, including feedbacks, that operate in the climate system and that will shape its response to additional GHG forcing.

This uncertainty is reflected in the conclusions that climate scientists reach about future climate change. When such conclusions are quantitative, they remain imprecise, just as we saw with conclusions about human contributions to recent warming in Section 3. For example, in their Fifth Assessment Report (AR5), the IPCC concluded that, for the moderately high emission scenario known as RCP6.0, global temperature during 2081–2100 would *likely* (probability ≥ 66 percent) be between 1.4 and 3.1°C warmer than during 1986–2005 (Collins et al. 2013). Similarly, in their Sixth Assessment Report (AR6), the IPCC found: "Compared to the recent past (1995–2014), GSAT [Global Surface Air Temperature] averaged over the period 2081–2100 is *very likely* to be higher by 0.2°C–1.0°C in the low-emissions scenario SSP1-1.9 and by 2.4°C–4.8°C in the high-emissions scenario SSP5-8.5" (Lee et al. 2021, p. 555).

This section examines how climate scientists arrive at such conclusions about future climate conditions. Section 4.1 discusses the use of ensembles of climate models to make projections and introduces the IPCC's default approach to inferring conclusions about future climate from those projections. Section 4.2 considers the epistemic significance of robustness in projections from the latest generation of models, while Section 4.3 discusses the significance of robustness across generations of models. Section 4.4 explains why and how climate science is beginning to move away from the default approach's "model democracy," where each climate model is given equal weight in the analysis. Section 4.5 briefly introduces an alternative approach to characterizing future climate change that does not rely on ensemble results. Finally, Section 4.6 considers the management of inductive risk in investigations of future climate change.

4.1 Ensembles and Their Interpretation

Paradigmatic climate variables, like global temperature, are shaped by causal processes unfolding not just in earth's atmosphere, but also in its oceans, on the land surface, in its ice sheets, and more. The relevant processes are numerous, interactive, nonlinear, and operate on a range of spatial and temporal scales. How best to model such a complex system depends in part on one's aims. For some purposes, it is fine, or even advantageous, to use highly simplified models that abstract away from most of the details. Energy-balance models, for instance, represent the climate system as a single point (or a small set of points) that is receiving radiation from the sun and emitting radiation back to space; nevertheless, they are useful for some purposes and have the advantage of being very computationally efficient. For many questions about the future that climate scientists seek to answer, however, such as questions about regional climate change, such simple models are clearly inadequate. Instead, climate scientists employ the complex GCMs and ESMs introduced in Section 3, which represent a wide range of causal processes and their interactions within a three-dimensional climate system.

There are a few dozen state-of-the-art GCMs/ESMs in use at modeling centers around the world today. Though they differ some in their details, these models are all of the same broad type: They are all informed by the same basic theoretical resources, and they all take a reductive approach to modeling the climate system, that is, one that aims to simulate the emergence of system-level properties from smaller-scale causal processes and components. Their differences reflect alternative choices in model development from within a shared modeling paradigm (see also Lloyd 2015). Typically, these differences are to be found in the range of causal processes represented, the way that sub-grid processes are parameterized, the numerical methods used to solve equations, the spacing of grid points, and/or the geometry of spatial grids. These differences stem from variations in modeling groups' expertise, interests, computational and personnel resources, and other factors.

GCMs/ESMs are a key resource in the study of future climate change. They are used both individually and collectively – as an *ensemble* – to explore what climate would be like under different greenhouse gas emission scenarios. Most notably, in support of the assessments of the IPCC, most major modeling groups around the world participate in periodic coupled model intercomparison projects (CMIPs) (see, e.g., Eyring et al. 2016). In these CMIPs, modeling groups use their latest GCMs/ESMs to perform a specified set of simulations, including simulations of past periods and of future periods under particular GHG emission scenarios, and then deposit results from these simulations in a shared database. In the last few IPCC assessment cycles, results from the latest CMIP, and published research analyzing them, have served as the foundation for the IPCC's efforts to draw conclusions about future climate change.

How to interpret sets of projections from climate model ensembles has been the subject of extensive debate. An epistemically conservative option is to understand the results to indicate *possibilities* for the future that cannot be ruled out, given today's understanding (Katzav 2014; Betz 2015; Katzav et al. 2021). Thus, if CMIP models project global mean temperature changes ranging from 1.4 to 3.1°C for a particular scenario, then warming in the range of 1.4– 3.1°C under that scenario cannot be ruled out; the ensemble indicates a "non-discountable envelope" (Stainforth et al. 2007) of global temperature change for the scenario. Whether warming outside the envelope is also possible is a further, separate matter. Another option is to interpret the collection of modeling results as a sample from a distribution of results, which stands in some relation to a *probability distribution* over future climate states, that is, a distribution indicating which climate conditions are more/less likely under the scenario. Various methods for producing such probability distributions have been developed and applied, involving different underlying assumptions about the ensemble of models (see Parker 2018 for examples and discussion).

Both types of interpretation have faced criticism. Probabilistic interpretations are criticized for resting on assumptions about the ensemble that either are known to be false – for example, that the ensemble is a random draw from a space of plausible models – or are such that it is uncertain whether they hold. The worry is that the probability distributions generated via these methods have a false precision and might be significantly misleading (Parker and Risbey 2015; Katzav et al. 2021). Possibilistic interpretations, however, are seen as relatively unhelpful to decision makers (Frame et al. 2007) and as understating what is known about future climate change (Risbey 2007; see Dethier 2023b for a broad critique of possibilistic interpretations).

The IPCC has taken a pragmatic approach in its recent assessment reports. For a given climate variable and a given scenario, the default approach has been to fit a Normal distribution to the set of changes projected by the latest CMIP ensemble, but then to interpret the central 5–95 percent of that distribution to indicate only a *likely* range, that is, a range into which the probability of the actual change falling is *at least 66 percent* (see Table 1 in Section 3.4). It was by applying this default approach in AR5 that the IPCC arrived at one of the conclusions reported above: For the moderate emission scenario known as RCP6.0, global mean temperature during 2081–2100 would *likely* be between 1.4 and 3.1°C warmer than during 1986–2005 (Collins et al. 2013).

The IPCC's default approach could be questioned in a number of respects (see Harris 2021, Ch.2; Winsberg 2018a, Ch.7). For instance, why fit a Normal distribution, as opposed to some other, to the results? Why downgrade only one likelihood category (from *very likely* to *likely*) rather than two (from *very likely* to *more likely than not*)? That said, it does have some attractive features. It occupies an epistemically intermediate position between possibilistic and (precise) probabilistic interpretations; imprecise probabilities, in the form of *likely* ranges, have the potential to avoid both false precision and substantially understating what is known. In addition, via downgrading, the default approach takes account – albeit in a coarse-grained way – of the fact that CMIP models, and ensembles of such models, have limitations that will introduce some error in their projections. Nevertheless, Section 4.4 will discuss a recent exception to the default approach and reasons to think that increasingly the default approach will be superseded.

4.2 Robustness Revisited

In addition to the ranges for global temperature change that have been the focus of discussion above, IPCC Working Group 1 (WG1) provides geographical maps of projected changes. In recent assessment reports, such maps typically show, for a grid of points at earth's surface, the average of the CMIP-projected changes for a given climate variable (like summer mean precipitation) as well as an indication of the extent to which the ensemble members agreed on the sign of the change and, in some cases, the extent to they agreed that the change would be significant in magnitude. A "significant" change here is one that exceeds a specified threshold of internal variability, the variability in climate conditions that occurs even in the absence of external forcing of the climate system.

Annual mean temperature change

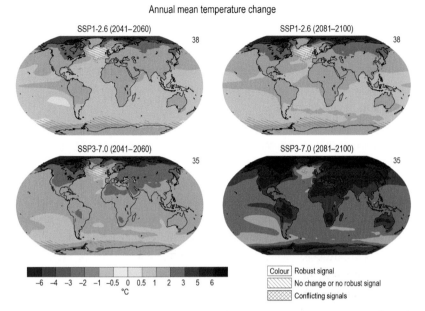

Figure 5 Projected multi-model average change in annual mean near-surface air temperature (Celsius) in 2041–2060 and 2081–2100 relative to 1995–2014 for two future scenarios (SSPs), along with information about model agreement. The number of climate models contributing projections is shown at the upper right of each panel. (Source: Figure 4.19 in IPCC 2021: Chapter 4. Reprinted with permission.)

In AR6, a *robust signal of change* in a variable at a grid point was reported only if both of the following conditions were met: At least 80 percent of the CMIP6 models agreed on the sign of the change of the variable at the grid point (making it "robust") and at least 66 percent of the CMIP6 models agreed that the magnitude of the change would be significant (indicating a "signal") (Lee et al. 2021). In Figure 5, the areas of the map that have no diagonal or crossed lines indicate grid points where these criteria were met for projected changes in annual mean temperature under a relatively low (SSP1-2.6) and a relatively high (SSP3-7.0) greenhouse gas emission scenario. As the figure shows, for annual mean temperature change, there are many grid points where the IPCC's criteria are met. On maps for many other variables, however, including variables related to precipitation and humidity, robust signals of change at the grid point level are rarer.[23]

---

[23] In some cases where projections indicate that no signal would have emerged at the grid point level by a given future date, such a signal is *already* emerging on aggregate/larger spatial scales in observations. Questions about the appropriate spatial scale(s) at which to analyze projections will be bracketed for this discussion. The general points to be made below about robustness hold regardless of the scale of analysis.

IPCC WG1 does not claim that such agreement among CMIP models has any particular epistemic significance; they simply show where projected changes by the CMIP ensemble do / do not display the specified levels of agreement. Nevertheless, in practice, such agreed-upon results often are taken to be ones that are relatively likely to be correct or that merit high confidence (see Pirtle et al. 2010). Is this justified?

Unsurprisingly, there is a debate here too. Wendy Parker (2011) argues that agreed-upon results from ensembles merit high confidence only under an assumption about climate model reliability that is often difficult to justify. Corey Dethier (2024) counters that, in the absence of specific evidence to the contrary, it is reasonable to assume that this reliability requirement *is* met, at least for binary (yes/no) questions. This is not only because core parts of climate models are constructed from accepted physical theory but also because, if there are types of question on which the models are unreliable – that is, where their answers are *anti*-correlated with truth – evidence of this is likely to be uncovered during the significant vetting process that they undergo. Eric Winsberg (2018a) carves out something of a middle ground, drawing on Schupbach's (2018) explanatory account of robustness analysis, discussed earlier in Section 2. He argues that whether robust climate modeling results lend strong support to a hypothesis depends on whether they jointly serve to rule out enough of the relevant competing hypotheses; he emphasizes that this will vary with the hypothesis under consideration and that results from sources other than models also play important roles in ruling out competitors.

No attempt will be made to evaluate these different positions here, though it is worth noting that they are not necessarily inconsistent with one another. The aims of this section are instead: First, to show that features of practice here are strongly suggestive of a jury theorem / wisdom of crowds perspective on CMIP ensembles, rather than one where additional ensemble members serve to rule out particular competing explanations; second, to explain from this jury theorem perspective why it makes sense that the IPCC does not attribute any particular epistemic significance to "robust" results; and, third, to show why nevertheless checking for strong agreement among models can in principle be epistemically valuable. This will culminate in the articulation of a form of robustness analysis that is distinct from Schupbach's explanatory variety.[24]

It is helpful to begin with an example of a jury theorem. According to Cordorcet's Jury Theorem (CJT), the probability that the majority opinion on

---

[24] Ryan O'Laughlin (2021) also appeals to practices in climate science to challenge the generality of Schupbach's account. He argues that Elisabeth Lloyd's (2015) "model robustness" gives a better account of how robustness considerations increase scientists' confidence that climate models adequately represent important causal processes.

a binary question is correct exceeds 0.5, and in the limit converges to 1, as the number of voters increases, provided that the voters are competent and vote independently, that is, provided that they each have probability $r > 0.5$ of indicating the correct answer and that the probability that one voter errs is not higher when some other voter errs (see, e.g., Dietrich and Speakerman 2021). Similar results can be proven when relaxing these competence and independence requirements to some extent, for example, to allow for some dependence among votes and for variation in competence across voters. Jury theorems entail that, under the right conditions, when a majority of voters chooses one answer to a binary question of interest rather than the other, this can be evidence – even quite powerful evidence – for the majority answer.

In a number of salient respects, analysis of CMIP projections aligns with the jury theorem framework. First, and most strikingly, climate scientists themselves often characterize CMIP models as *voters*; they refer to the default practice of giving equal weight to projections from CMIP models as "model democracy" or "one model, one vote" (Knutti 2010; Lee et al. 2021). Second, the questions about future climate change for which the IPCC typically performs robustness analysis are *binary* questions about the sign and significance of projected changes, as noted earlier. Third, robustness analysis of CMIP projections is concerned with whether a sufficient *majority* of models agrees on the sign and/or magnitude of a future climate change, without regard for which models voted which way. Finally, climate scientists recognize *dependence* among models as a factor that complicates their analysis and have investigated its extent, for example, as indicated by correlated errors in simulations of past climate. These investigations show that some CMIP models exhibit strong dependence – especially when they are variants of the same model developed by a single modeling group – and that consequently the effective number of climate models/voters is often much smaller than the actual number, perhaps only on the order of a dozen or so (see, e.g., Pennell and Reichler 2011; Masson and Knutti 2011).

Yet IPCC WG1 does not appeal to a jury theorem like the CJT to argue that agreed-upon CMIP results are likely to be correct and, indeed, refrains from attributing any particular epistemic significance to such results, as noted earlier. This is readily explained, however, by the fact that average model/voter *competence* is expected to vary significantly with the type of questions about future climate change being asked (i.e., which variable, timescale, scenario, region, threshold, etc.), is significantly uncertain for many questions, and for some types of question might be quite low ($r \sim 0.5$) or even absent entirely ($r < 0.5$). Prime candidates for the latter are questions that ask about changes in a variable under scenarios and/or on timescales where the change will often be close to the threshold that distinguishes different answers, for example, close to the internal variability threshold that marks "significant" change. For these types of question, which are not always easy to identify in advance, even a relatively small bias shared by many of the CMIP models – due to a poorly represented second-order process, for example – could be enough to push their average reliability below 0.5, that is, to render them *in*competent.

It is thus unsurprising that IPCC WG1 emphasized in AR5 that confidence or likelihood statements cannot be derived from model agreement alone, without considering model dependence as well as factors indicative of model competence, such as relevant performance in simulating past climate change and the degree to which the physical processes that will drive the change in the particular variable of interest are thought to be well understood and well represented in the models (see Collins et al. 2013, p. 1043). Performing this sort of tailored assessment of dependence and competence/reliability, however, is outside the IPCC's remit, insofar as it would amount to conducting significant new research. It would also be prohibitively time-consuming for the IPCC, given the many models participating in CMIPs and the many variables, scenarios, etc., for which CMIP results are presented in IPCC reports. Moreover, given the brevity of the observational record available for testing the models, we can expect that substantial uncertainty about how reliable models are (when it comes to answering particular types of question about future climate change) will remain even after such assessment efforts. Ultimately, tailored assessment of model dependence and reliability, of a sort that might underwrite inferences from model agreement to conclusions about likelihood or confidence, is hard work left for climate researchers to do outside of the IPCC process and is only beginning to be performed (see Section 4.4.)

Even in the absence of such assessment, however, it can make sense to investigate levels of agreement among CMIP models/voters. This is because *patterns of agreement and disagreement in voting outcomes can themselves be powerful evidence regarding model/voter reliability.* This can be illustrated from the perspective of various accounts of evidence. Here, a Bayesian perspective will be adopted, where evidence favors a hypothesis over a rival to the extent that the evidence would be more likely to occur if the hypothesis is true than if the rival is true (see also Section 2.3). Two assumptions about models/voters will be important to the argument. First, it is assumed that, except for perhaps a small minority, most models/voters have similar reliability. Second it is assumed that the ensemble of models/voters has an effective size of at least half a dozen models/voters, that is, that the dependence among their votes on the type of question at hand is not so great that the ensemble functions like just a few independent models/voters.

Keeping in mind these assumptions, consider three exhaustive hypotheses regarding the reliability, r, of typical models/voters for binary questions of a given type, $\{q\}$. The hypotheses concern the value of $r_{\{q\}}$, the frequency with which typical model/voters would answer correctly when asked binary questions of type $\{q\}$:

H_{high}:   Models/voters are highly competent for $\{q\}$, that is, $r_{\{q\}} \gg 0.5$.

H_{mid}:   Models/voters have only middling reliability for $\{q\}$, that is, $\sim(r_{\{q\}} \gg 0.5$ or $r_{\{q\}} \ll 0.5)$.

H_{low}:   Models/voters are very unreliable for $\{q\}$, that is, $r_{\{q\}} \ll 0.5$.

For purposes of illustration, let's suppose that a question is of type $\{q\}$ if it asks about the sign of the change in average summer rainfall that would occur by the late twenty-first century at a midlatitude grid point under a moderate or high emission scenario. Suppose that the voting outcome that we observe on some question of type $\{q\}$ – concerning one model grid point – is strong majority agreement among ensemble members that rainfall would decrease. This will count as some (Bayesian) evidence in favor of H_{high} and H_{low} and against H_{mid}, because strong majority outcomes are likely if H_{high} or H_{low} is true and unlikely if H_{mid} is true. Strong majority outcomes are likely if H_{high} (H_{low}) is true because highly competent (very unreliable) voters almost always answer correctly (incorrectly) and thus almost always agree. If, when numerous questions of type $\{q\}$ are considered, near unanimous agreement is almost always observed, this will be strong evidence against H_{mid}, because such a set of outcomes is very unlikely if H_{mid} is true. Conversely, slim majority outcomes are likely if H_{mid} is true and are unlikely if H_{high} or H_{low} is true; they are evidence for H_{mid}. Finding that slim majority outcomes are the norm across many questions sampled from $\{q\}$ will be strong evidence for H_{mid} and against both H_{high} and H_{low}.[25]

This evidence regarding $r_{\{q\}}$ can be quite useful if one's goal is *to identify answers that are very likely to be correct*. First, consider the case where slim majority outcomes are found to be the norm. Continuing with our example, suppose a large number of midlatitude grid points are checked, and at most grid points only a slim majority of CMIP models agrees on the sign of the change in summer rainfall. Bayesian updating on this evidence will redistribute to H_{mid} nearly all of the prior probability mass that had been assigned to H_{high} and H_{low}; the probability assigned to H_{mid} will approach 1. But if H_{mid} is true, then it will be unclear whether $r_{\{q\}}$ exceeds 0.5 and, even if it does, the probability that the

---

[25] Finding that intermediate levels of agreement are the norm for $\{q\}$ will fail to clearly discriminate between H_{mid} and H_{high} (or H_{low}). And a bimodal distribution – where we almost always see either a very strong majority or a slim majority, and rarely something in between – suggests that what was thought to be one question type actually encompasses two (or more).

majority answer is correct may not be very high. In this situation, the pattern of agreement does *not* constitute good evidence that majority answers to questions of type {q} are "very likely to be correct."

Next, consider the case where near unanimous outcomes are found to be the norm. Bayesian updating on this evidence will redistribute to H_{high} and H_{low} nearly all of the prior probability mass that had been assigned to H_{mid}. Whether the updated probability for H_{high} reaches some desired threshold (say, for acceptance of H_{high}) will depend on both how the prior probability mass was distributed among H_{high}, H_{mid}, and H_{low} and how high the acceptance threshold is. Notably, in situations where uncertainty about model/voter competence is primarily about whether H_{high} or H_{mid} is correct (i.e., H_{low} is antecedently deemed very unlikely), the vast majority of the redistributed probability will go to H_{high}, and a desired threshold for acceptance of H_{high} might well be reached.[26] And then from H_{high} it will follow, by Condorcet-type reasoning, that whichever answer receives the majority of votes *is* very likely to be correct.

At this point, we are in a position to articulate a form of robustness analysis (RA) that is distinct from Schupbach's explanatory variety and that is motivated by *uncertainty about source reliability*. It is applicable in situations where the assumptions noted at the outset are met: Most sources are expected to have relatively similar reliability (though there is uncertainty about what that reliability is) and the effective size of the source pool is not too small. In *voting RA*, the analyst checks whether, when answering binary questions of a given type, a set of sources exhibits strong majority agreement with a frequency that is consistent with their having a desired high level of competence, r*, and inconsistent with their having a more middling level of reliability. The value of r*, and the thresholds defining consistency/inconsistency, are determined by how strongly the analyst wants to avoid concluding that sources are highly competent on binary questions of a given type – and thus that their answers are very likely to be correct – when this is false, that is, how strongly she wants to avoid Type I errors.[27] An informal variety of voting RA can be performed by simply checking whether sources generally exhibit nearly unanimous agreement when answering a given type of binary question, without specifying a precise value for r* or performing any calculations. At a minimum, finding such agreement

---

[26] Recall Bayes' Theorem: $p(H|e) = p(e|H)/p(e)*p(H)$. If $p(e|H)/p(e)$ is the same for two hypotheses, then the increase in their probabilities in light of evidence e will be proportional to their priors. Here, this condition is met, i.e., $p(e|H_{high})/p(e) = p(e|H_{low})/p(e)$. If the prior for H_{high} is much larger than the prior for H_{low}, its proportional increase is, in absolute terms, much larger. For example, if $p(H_{high}) = 0.48$ and $p(H_{low}) = 0.01$, then H_{high} will receive 48 times (!) more of the probability redistributed from H_{mid}.

[27] For example, the analyst very concerned to avoid Type I errors could choose r* such that sources need to usually display unanimity or near unanimity.

will allow the analyst to limit attention to questions and answers where the behavior of the voting pool is *consistent with* high competence. In situations where it is antecedently deemed very implausible that sources are very unreliable (i.e., where H_{low} is antecedently deemed very implausible), finding such agreement will constitute strong (Bayesian) evidence that sources are highly competent and thus that their majority answers to questions of that type are very likely to be correct.[28]

While it is theoretically promising, the extent to which voting RA can be successfully applied in the context of climate change projection remains to be seen. There are difficult reference class issues that need to be addressed, related to the individuation of question types. In addition, voting RA is premised on the two conditions specified at the outset – that most models have similar reliability and that their votes aren't too dependent – and it is not clear how often it will be reasonable to assume that those conditions hold for CMIP models. Even when they are thought to hold for a given type of question about future climate change, epistemic progress via voting RA will depend on which patterns of agreement actually occur in CMIP projections; at present, strong majority agreement tends to occur for questions that climate scientists could *already* confidently answer, even before the latest CMIP results were produced. Finally, it remains to be seen how often H_{low} can be assigned a very low prior probability for climate models and how such assignments should be determined.[29] Yet, however these matters turn out, it is worth keeping in mind, and looking for opportunities to apply, the simple insight underlying voting RA: that sometimes the extent of agreement among scientific models is itself evidence regarding their reliability.

4.3 Intergenerational Robustness

It was just noted that strong majority agreement among the latest CMIP models tends to occur for questions that climate scientists could already confidently answer. Questions about the sign and significance of long-term changes in annual mean temperature under scenarios involving additional large increases in greenhouse gas concentrations are good examples (see Figure 5). That, in most locales, these changes will be positive in sign and will far exceed the thresholds of internal

---

[28] Similar considerations are leveraged by Bovens and Hartmann (2004, Ch.3) in the context of a different argument related to voter reliability.

[29] If they are determined entirely subjectively, per some Bayesian approaches, then confidence in projections via voting RA could come too easily. Note, however, that voting RA can also be articulated in other evidential frameworks. In an error-statistical framework (Mayo 1996, 2018), for instance, H_{low} would presumably need to be ruled out via severe testing, whether formal or informal.

variability that make for "significant" change is supported by a host of consider-ations, including basic physical understanding of the climate system, theoretical analyses, changes already observed to occur, analysis of paleoclimate data, and results from previous generations of climate models. The same is true of the conclusion that, under moderate and high emission scenarios, global warming during the twenty-first century is very likely to exceed that of the twentieth century. As emphasized by Eric Winsberg (2018a, Ch.12), many important conclusions about future climate change are supported by diverse evidential sources – not just results from the latest CMIP models.

This, however, raises a question: What *is* the added value of projections from the latest generation of climate models? To answer this, let's consider how later generations of CMIP models differ from earlier ones. Most models in a later generation will be built upon models from the previous generation, but the newer models typically will represent some climate system processes with higher fidelity, will include representations of some processes that were left out of models in the previous generation, and will have fixes to some "bugs" found in the code of previous model versions. Some of the newer models might also have finer spatial resolution as well.

Because of these differences, the models in the newer generation are expected to be, in general, somewhat better bookkeepers than their predecessors – they are expected to do a better job of keeping track of the quantitative contributions of myriad interacting causal processes that determine how climate changes (see Section 3.2). An evaluation against past data typically reveals that newer models do perform somewhat better, on average or for the most part, across a range of climate variables. So, in part, the newer models add value by serving as additional, potentially higher-quality-on-average sources of information (i.e., voters) regarding future climate change.

In addition, insofar as newer models have finer spatial resolution, they present an opportunity to examine (simulated) processes and dynamics in finer detail, which may reveal interesting or surprising features worthy of further investigation or lead to new insights about how observed climate phenomena come about. Among their many other uses, three-dimensional climate models like GCMs/ESMs serve as surrogate climate systems for research purposes. Unlike for the real climate system, where observations are gappy in space and time, information about conditions in the simulated climate system is complete, in the sense that the researcher can access the values assigned to model variables at every grid point and during every time step of the simulation. Visualizations of these data can be made and studied just like observational data. Newer models with finer spatial resolution, and with add-itional physical processes represented, are richer surrogate systems to study.

Finally, insofar as some of the simplifications, omissions, and bugs of previous generations of models are addressed in the newer models, running the newer models also provides a means of testing how much those previous limitations mattered to the results. When a new generation of CMIP models projects changes in climate similar to those of the previous generation, this provides some reassurance regarding the earlier projections, by showing that those particular shortcomings didn't make much difference to the results. Here we see a kind of intergenerational robustness analysis (e.g., Knutti and Sedlacek 2013; Lee et al. 2021), where the logic *does* fit nicely with Schupbach's explanatory account. When the new generation of CMIP models gives projections similar to the previous generation's, this helps to eliminate hypotheses like (*H'*) *the sorts of changes projected by the previous generation were significantly biased due to the models' relatively simpler process representations, their omissions, their lower spatial resolution*, etc. This in turn warrants increased confidence in the hypothesis that (*H*) *the projected changes of the previous generation are relatively accurate*. The extent of the increase in confidence depends on how much probability had been accorded to *H'*. In practice, these increases are not quantified, but intergenerational agreement is recognized as epistemically valuable. For example, discussing patterns of temperature and precipitation change in results from the CMIP3 and CMIP5 ensembles, Knutti and Sedlaček (2013) remark:

> We argue that this robustness across generations of models is positive, and its consistency with simpler models, theoretical process understanding and observed changes provides strong support for the argument that climate change over the twenty-first century will probably exceed that observed over the past century, even for the RCP2.6 scenario in which global greenhouse-gas emissions are reduced by about 90% in 2100 compared with the present." (p. 369).

Given the long-accumulating variety of support for some conclusions about future climate change, if a new generation of CMIP models were found to project changes in climate that *disagreed* with those conclusions, suspicion might fall first on the new modeling results themselves. This is in fact what happened in the case of global temperature change projections from CMIP6, the models that informed the IPCC's AR6, as discussed in the next section.

4.4 Beyond Model Democracy

As explained in Section 4.1, the default IPCC approach to estimating future changes in climate has been to fit a Normal distribution to the set of changes projected by the latest CMIP ensemble, but then to interpret the central

5–95 percent of that distribution as only a *likely* range, that is, a range that has at least 66 percent probability of including the actual change that would occur (Lee et al. 2021, Box 4.1). This default approach involves a kind of "model democracy," insofar as each model is given equal weight in the analysis; each model's "vote" (i.e., estimate) regarding the changes in climate that would occur counts equally in arriving at conclusions.

There are both scientific and political reasons for the adoption of model democracy in climate science. Scientifically, it is difficult to quantify how much better one state-of-the-art climate model is than another for a given predictive task (Parker 2006; Knutti 2018). First, many CMIP models look to be of roughly similar quality from the perspective of model construction: They are of the same general type, attempting to represent a similar set of climate system processes, informed by the same physical theories, and with similar spatiotemporal resolution. Second, when it comes to model performance on past data, it is challenging to identify the most relevant performance metrics – indicators that a model will perform well in projecting a given future climate variable; typically, there will be various reasonable choices that can give somewhat different verdicts on which models are best. Adding to the challenge is the fact that reliable global-scale observations of climate conditions, against which such performance can be evaluated, are available only for the last century or so, which is very brief in climatological terms. Thus, in the absence of accepted methods for quantifying the relative quality of climate models, and given that multi-model average results often outperform individual models when compared to past observations (Gleckler et al. 2008; Eyring et al. 2021), equal weighting has remained the default.[30] Equal weighting is also convenient politically, insofar as it means that any climate models that are (unofficially) considered to be of lower quality – which might include the flagship models of particular countries – are not called out as such in IPCC analyses.

Over time, however, model democracy has come to seem increasingly problematic. When simulating past climate, some CMIP models perform significantly better than others in some respects, and some models exhibit above-average performance (relative to the ensemble) on a majority of commonly assessed climate variables (see, e.g., Gleckler et al. 2008; Eyring et al. 2021, Section 3.8.2). In addition, there are issues of double (or triple or more) counting of votes, given that some modeling centers contribute results from multiple models that are minor variations on one another. Consequently,

---

[30] Further support for this choice comes from demonstrations that incorrect weighting can easily make conclusions more inaccurate (Weigel et al. 2010).

between AR5 and AR6, some climate scientists began developing and applying methods for weighting projections, taking account of dependence among
models as well as model performance on metrics relevant to the projected
variable (see, e.g., Knutti et al. 2017). In addition, a new methodology for
reducing uncertainty in projections, known as "emergent constraints" (Hall
and Qu 2006; Heinze et al. 2019) was increasingly gaining traction. The
methodology of emergent constraints works by, first, identifying an observ-
able (measurable) feature of present climate that is controlled by the same
physical processes that are expected to control the future change of interest
and, second, excluding or down-weighting projections from models that fail to
simulate that feature of present climate in a way that is consistent with
observations.

A surprising turn of events created a high-profile opportunity for the application of these methods and led, finally, to a very limited move away from model
democracy by the IPCC in AR6 (IPCC 2021). As CMIP6 simulations were being
completed, it became clear that many of the models had projected significantly
greater warming than expected (Voosen 2021). These "hot models" also tended to
give climate sensitivity estimates well outside the 1.5–4.5°C *likely* range that had
been stable for decades, just as the most comprehensive analysis to date was
reaffirming that sensitivity > 4.5°C is unlikely (Sherwood et al. 2020).[31] Climate
scientists faced a dilemma. On the one hand, the temperature change projections
from the hot models were judged to be implausible, in light of theoretical
understanding, past observations, and previous generations of CMIP models.
On the other hand, the hot models, like the other CMIP6 models, had been
demonstrated to perform well overall across a familiar suite of performance
metrics (when simulating past climate) and, indeed, were considered an
improvement upon previous generations of models.

The dilemma appears to have its roots in a view of model quality that is
common in many sciences. Call it the *mirror view of model quality*, according
to which a model is of higher quality the closer it comes to accurately and
comprehensively representing a target system in some overall sense. (We saw
a close cousin of this view in the context of data modeling in Section 2.2.)
Typical model evaluation activities in climate science fit well with such
a view. For instance, to show how successive generations of CMIP models
have improved in quality, the IPCC highlights increases in model resolution
(i.e., level of detail of representation), comprehensiveness (i.e., range of
processes represented), and pattern correlation with observations across

---

[31] There are various conceptions of climate sensitivity. For present purposes, it can be thought of as
the long-term change in global temperature that would occur if atmospheric carbon dioxide
concentrations were instantaneously doubled from preindustrial levels.

a wide range of variables (i.e., general representational fidelity) (see Arias et al. 2021, Figure TS.2). The problem is that a model that looks to be of relatively good quality from the perspective of the mirror view – its mean or median performance across a set of variables is quite good – can nevertheless perform quite poorly in particular respects. Even for a single variable, poor performance in specific time periods or regimes can be partially masked when evaluation considers a model's average error over a longer time period or multiple regimes.

It appears that this partial masking of poor performance is what happened in the case of the hot models. Given the perceived implausibility of the hot models' temperature projections, some groups of climate researchers carried out additional tests that aimed to probe the models' ability to simulate, specifically, how global temperature responds to increasing greenhouse gas concentrations. For example, one test compared simulated and observed temperature trends for the period 1981–2017, when greenhouse gas levels, but not other climate drivers, were changing significantly (Tokarska et al. 2020). Many of the hot models were found to perform poorly on such tests. Using emergent constraints and other weighting methodologies, the poor-performing models were omitted or down-weighted when estimating future temperature changes in these studies (see Figure 6).

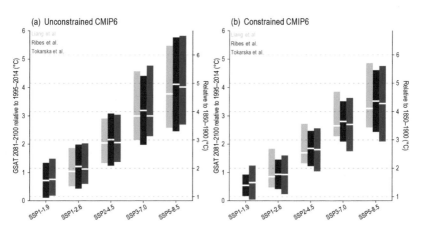

Figure 6 For several different emission scenarios (SSPs), unconstrained and constrained 5–95 percent ranges of global surface air temperature (GSAT) change by the late twenty-first century from three CMIP6 studies: Liang et al. 2020 (left bars), Ribes et al. 2021 (middle bars), and Tokarska et al. 2020 (right bars). The unconstrained ranges differ somewhat because the studies used different subsamples of the CMIP6 archive. (Source: Figure 4.11 Panel (a) and Panel (b) in IPCC 2021: Chapter 4. Reprinted with permission.)

The resulting estimates were similar to those derived from the previous generation of CMIP models and in line with expectations (Voosen 2021).[32]

These studies involving down-weighting of models subsequently played an important role in AR6. Rather than following the usual practice of model democracy, the IPCC provided "assessed warming" ranges for each scenario by averaging the 5–95 percent ranges from three studies that down-weighted some of the hot models (see Figure 6) and then averaging this with the 5–95 percent range derived from a simpler model ("emulator") run with observationally consistent parameters (see Lee et al. 2021, Section 4.3.4 for details). This assessed warming range for each scenario was judged *very likely* (probability ≥90 percent) to include the actual change that would occur. Examples of such ranges were given earlier in this section: "Compared to the recent past (1995–2014), GSAT [Global Surface Air Temperature] averaged over the period 2081–2100 is *very likely* to be higher by 0.2°C–1.0°C in the low-emissions scenario SSP1-1.9 and by 2.4°C–4.8°C in the high-emissions scenario SSP5-8.5" (Lee et al. 2021, p.555).

The more focused tests that climate scientists carried out in response to the hot model projections align with an alternative perspective on model quality, a *fitness-for-purpose view* (see also Section 2.2). On this view, models are *tools* (Knuuttila 2011; Currie 2018), and the quality of a model is greater to the extent that it can be used successfully for a specified purpose of interest (Parker 2009, 2020). Evaluation of model fitness-for-purpose consequently takes a more tailored form than evaluation under the mirror view, focusing on those aspects of the construction and performance of a model that are most relevant to the achievement of the purpose of interest. This is precisely how emerging methodologies used for weighting or culling climate model projections work. Rather than considering how a climate model performs in some general or overall sense, these methods employ weighting criteria or exclusion tests that are specific to a particular projected variable, often related to the physical processes that are expected control changes in that projected variable (Knutti et al. 2017; see also Carrier and Lenhard 2019; Kawamleh 2022).

Climate scientists are increasingly adopting a fitness-for-purpose perspective on model evaluation (see, e.g., Baumberger et al. 2017; IPCC 2021, Ch.1 and Ch.10). But fitness-for-purpose evaluation involves challenges that mirror-view evaluation does not. Rather than just one general, purpose-neutral model evaluation exercise, which documents model performance across a broad suite of

---

[32] While what caused many CMIP6 models to "run hot" continues to be investigated, it is thought to be related to changes in the representation of cloud processes. See, e.g., Zelinka et al. (2020).

familiar performance metrics, each predictive and explanatory purpose requires its own tailored evaluation exercise.[33] This tailored evaluation needs to consider (among other things) which metrics of performance are most relevant to the purpose at hand and how much weight each metric should be given; as noted earlier, often there will be various reasonable choices that can give somewhat different verdicts on which models are best. In light of these and other challenges, there is so far no consensus on how best to move beyond model democracy. The IPCC accordingly continued to employ model democracy in the AR6, except for a few variables for which multiple weighting studies had given relatively similar results. They explained: "For other quantities [besides changes in global surface temperature, ocean warming and sea level], such robust methods do not yet exist to constrain the projections" (IPCC 2021, Summary for Policymakers, p.12). Perhaps this will have changed by the time the next IPCC assessment is completed.

4.5 Storylines and Tales

The discussion so far has focused on future changes in climate as indicated by ensembles of global climate models. The spatial resolution of GCMs/ESMs, however, remains rather coarse; as noted earlier, surface grid points might be spaced 100 km in the horizontal. Such models cannot simulate small-scale impactful weather phenomena, nor can they simulate sharp variations in conditions that occur at smaller scales, for example, variations in precipitation amounts due to orography or shorelines. They are not ideal tools for obtaining accurate information about future changes in climate at the local and regional scales that matter to people's lives.

A standard way of proceeding in the face of these limitations of global models is to "downscale" GCM/ESM results. Downscaling comes in two main varieties. Statistical downscaling involves identifying statistical relationships between a GCM/ESM's grid point values and observed local weather conditions in past periods and then applying those relationships to the GCM/ ESM's grid point values for future times. Dynamical downscaling involves running a higher-resolution regional climate model where the boundary conditions for the simulation are taken from global models' simulations of future conditions. Both approaches can be used to produce estimates of changes in climate conditions at finer spatial scales, but each has potential limitations as well: Model-observation relationships that hold for past periods may fail to hold for future ones, and conditions simulated by regional climate models may be inconsistent with those simulated by the global models that provided the

---

[33] I owe the language of "purpose-neutral" evaluation to Donal Khosrowi (personal communication).

regional models' boundary conditions. In addition, downscaled results, like GCM/ESM results, are often communicated in the form of maps showing average projected changes or else as probability distributions over future conditions, which tends to focus attention on mean and median changes, rather than low-probability high-impact changes that may be important to consider in adaptation decision making.

In part because of limitations of the standard approaches, increasingly climate scientists are employing complementary "storyline" approaches to providing climate information at regional and local scales (Shepherd 2019; Lee et al. 2021). Storyline approaches encompass a somewhat heterogeneous set of activities, but they have in common that they characterize weather or climate conditions in one possible future climate state, rather than giving a statistical summary of the future states projected by an ensemble. Oftentimes, the possible future state that is chosen is a relatively extreme one that is estimated to have a low probability of occurring but would be very impactful if it were to occur. It might be chosen by examining a set of projections from global or regional models and selecting one that shows among the largest changes in a set of climate variables of interest. These future conditions are typically characterized not only using maps and quantitative data, but also via narrative descriptions. In addition, storylines often relate projected changes to societal impacts of interest and sometimes contextualize the changes by comparing them to past events or conditions experienced in the locale.

Some storyline approaches focus on particular weather situations relevant to climate adaptation and planning. For example, Hazeleger et al. (2015) envision "tales of future weather" that are produced by running a high-resolution weather forecasting model to simulate a familiar impactful weather event (e.g., a heavy rainfall, a heatwave, or a hurricane) but with boundary conditions – such as sea surface temperatures – from a future climate state. The simulated event can then be compared to the past event already experienced, for example, the simulation indicates that 40 percent more rainfall would have fallen, which in turn can be translated into impacts of interest, for example, regarding the extent of the resulting flooding. As this suggests, the "tales" approach calls for tailoring the analysis to the particular outcomes and impacts that matter to the decision makers or stakeholders for whom the analysis is being performed.

4.6 Uncertainty, Inductive Risk, and Values

In Section 4.2, voting RA assumed that the goal of robustness analysis was to identify projected changes that would be *very likely to occur* under a given scenario. This goal reflects a particular inductive risk orientation that is common in science, namely, one that prioritizes avoidance of Type I errors, which involve accepting a hypothesis that is false. It is considered better to be epistemically cautious – to hold off on accepting a hypothesis, in effect suspending judgment, until very strong evidence is available, than to accept a hypothesis in light of preliminary evidence in its favor. Yet suspending judgment is not without costs. In the context of climate projection, the hypotheses under consideration assert that particular changes in climate would occur under a given scenario or will actually occur in the near term. If some of these hypotheses are true, but there is a long delay in accepting (and reporting) them as scientists wait for evidence to grow from moderately strong to very strong, there could be serious negative consequences. For example, a community might suffer costly and deadly flooding in the coming decades, because they were unaware that precipitation events were likely to become much more intense in their region and so did not factor this in when making infrastructure choices. How such *non-epistemic* considerations do and should shape climate science practice, including its methodologies and its standards of evidence, is increasingly a topic of discussion among philosophers and climate scientists (see, e.g., Lloyd and Oreskes 2018; Knutson et al. 2019; Shepherd 2019; Undorf et al. 2022; Pulkkinen et al. 2022).

Eric Winsberg (2018a) has argued that there are non-epistemic values "in the nooks and crannies" of the climate models used to project future climate change. This is because non-epistemic values shape the selection of predictive priorities, that is, which conditions are considered most important to accurately predict, and thereby the course of model development and the results produced. For example, given a modeling group's predictive priorities at time t – which might or might not be explicitly stated and documented – the group might work to improve the model's representation of process A, whereas with a different set of priorities they would have focused their efforts on process B. Changes made in the model's representation of process A, in turn, will constrain some future choices in model development. After years or even decades of model development involving many scientists, the results produced by a given climate model will be the net effect of myriad such choices, with the motivation for many of the choices unknown to current modelers (Biddle and Winsberg 2010; Winsberg 2018b). The upshot is that both results from individual climate models and estimates of uncertainty produced using ensembles of climate models are shaped in subtle and often unrecognized ways by value-mediated choices in model development (Winsberg 2018b; Parker and Winsberg 2018).

Winsberg (2018a, Ch. 9) emphasizes that this sort of value influence is not one that should raise worries of "wishful thinking," where value influence serves to systematically bias research toward some preferred conclusion.

Nevertheless, he and Wendy Parker argue that it may be problematic in other respects (Parker and Winsberg 2018). In particular, it may serve to perpetuate existing inequalities, both epistemic and practical. This is because it is not uncommon for modeling groups to prioritize accurate prediction of conditions *in their own countries and regions*, and most modeling groups are located in rich, Northern countries. As a consequence, these countries are likely to end up with higher-quality information about their future climate conditions and thus to be in a relatively better position to prepare. Conversely, poorer communities that lack modeling resources are likely to end up with lower-quality information, involving larger uncertainties, leaving them in a relatively worse position to prepare. To help prevent these sorts of epistemic and practical inequalities, Julie Jebeile and Michel Crucifix (2021) propose that the development and evaluation of climate models should be informed by a diversity of standpoints and values (see also Leuschner 2015).

Ahmed Elabbar (2023) develops a related, justice-based argument for varying evidential standards in the context of scientific assessments like those conducted by the IPCC. His argument begins from the contingent fact that there is background evidential inequality: Many more studies and analyses of present and future climate change are produced for the Global North than for the Global South. Elabbar argues that, given this evidential inequality, maintaining fixed high evidential standards – where very strong evidence is required before a finding is accepted and reported – will result in an unequal distribution of "epistemic power" in scientific assessments: A higher rate of findings will be produced for stakeholders in evidence-rich regions than will be produced for those in evidence-poor regions. He contends that, insofar as such inequalities of epistemic power will disadvantage those in evidence-poor regions with respect to fundamental interests, such as basic human rights, this is a strong reason in favor of varying evidential standards in scientific assessments. Elabbar's argument would allow for less stringent standards both for what counts as evidence *at all* in a scientific assessment (e.g., perhaps non-peer-reviewed grey literature can count) and for what counts as *enough* evidence for a finding to be reported. A risk of significantly more intense precipitation events in some regions of Africa, for example, might be reported even when there is only preliminary evidence supporting that conclusion.

While Elabbar argues for varying evidential standards insofar as this facilitates greater equality of epistemic power in a scientific assessment, a more radical proposal would be to adopt, more generally, lower evidential standards for asserting the presence of a climate risk or a risk of a given magnitude. Put differently, climate scientists could choose to prioritize the avoidance of Type II errors, which involve a failure to report (or an underestimation of) a real climate risk/change. Although prioritizing avoidance of Type II errors is uncommon in the sciences, it is accepted practice in some applied scientific contexts – like medical screening – where the practical consequences of such errors are particularly bad. The question has been raised whether, given the stakes, the investigation of future changes in climate ought to be more like medical screening than physics in this regard (Lloyd and Oreskes 2018; Lloyd et al. 2021). Indeed, the very aims of (this part of) climate science might be reconceived, like those of medical screening, to go beyond the purely epistemic to include, for example, protecting human well-being or advancing human security (Lee 2021; see also Adams et al. 2015). Prioritizing avoidance of Type II errors when investigating future climate risks/changes could then be justified insofar as it serves the aims of (this part of) climate science as a practice.

One might worry, however, that lowering evidential standards for asserting the presence of a climate risk could compromise the broader credibility of climate science. In fact, arguments made by Stephen John (2016) suggest that, if climate science lowers its standards for assertion, it could be *reasonable* for many people to fail to defer to climate scientists' testimony regarding climate change. John contends that it can be reasonable for a person to fail to defer to expert testimony when the expert's standard for assertion (i.e., the strength of evidence they require before asserting p) is weaker than the person's standard for acceptance (i.e., the strength of evidence they require before accepting that p). The latter may depend on the person's values, including their political commitments; to the extent that a person judges that the consequences of erroneously accepting that p would be particularly bad, she may rationally have a more demanding standard for acceptance.[34] According to John, however, the IPCC currently has a standard for assertion so demanding that almost nobody will have an even more demanding standard for acceptance, even if they strongly value, say, economic growth. So, although many people do fail to defer to IPCC testimony, almost nobody is currently justified in doing so, at least not on grounds of having a more demanding standard of acceptance (John 2016). If this argument is right, then prioritizing avoidance of Type II errors might make it reasonable, going forward, for more people to fail to accept what climate scientists report about future climate risks.

Yet perhaps this concern is not so serious. Headline claims of the IPCC concerning the existence of climate change, humans' role in it, and continued future warming have already been reached under demanding standards of assertion. So, skepticism about those key claims would remain unreasonable if, going forward, climate science were to adopt methods that carried a greater

---

[34] We saw a similar claim above by Reiss (2015); see Section 3.4.

risk of Type I error when investigating climate risks. The more serious concern instead seems to be the possibility of a broad, *unwarranted* loss of credibility for climate science, such that more people discount or ignore even very well-supported claims about climate change.

A less radical proposal that would also avoid concerns about loss of credibility has been offered by Elisabeth Lloyd and co-authors (2021). The IPCC assessments tend to report conclusions that the experts judged to be *likely* (≥66 percent probability) or *very likely* (≥90 percent probability) in light of the available evidence. Nearby conclusions – in particular conclusions judged *more likely than not* (>50 percent probability) – are not routinely reported and, indeed, are not a standard target of assessment. Lloyd et al. suggest that routinely providing a range of conclusions in light of the available evidence – reporting what is *more likely than not*, what is *likely*, and what is *very likely* – would be more useful, given the different information needs of decision makers in different contexts. Lloyd et al. point to the legal context in particular, where "more likely than not" is often the relevant standard of proof. Following Lloyd et al.'s proposal would create more work for scientists, but it has real advantages. Most notably, reporting a range of conclusions at different likelihood levels would serve a more diverse set of inductive risk preferences and would not require building specific non-epistemic values into climate science as a field.

5 Conclusion

The preceding sections have examined how contemporary climate scientists have addressed three central questions about climate change: To what extent is earth's climate warming? What is causing this warming? What will climate be like in the future? In doing so, it has provided a glimpse – but only a glimpse – of the epistemology of climate science today. Even so, some general features begin to come into view.

The central roles of computational models. While this feature of the epistemology of climate science was emphasized already in Section 1, the sections that followed demonstrated just how central computer simulation is to the practice of climate science today. We saw that computational models are essential resources both for developing quantitative explanations of climate phenomena and for projecting future climate change. They also serve as surrogate climate systems for research purposes, providing complete gridded results that can be analyzed like observational data to gain insights into climate phenomena. They are even employed in some efforts to estimate changes in global temperature, when reanalysis methods, which combine information from observations and simulations, are used. Much of what is learned about the climate system and climate change is mediated by computational modeling.

Diverse lines of evidence and robustness. The importance of computational modeling notwithstanding, conclusions in which climate scientists have high confidence typically have multiple, diverse lines of support. The conclusion that earth's climate is warming significantly is supported by diverse observations of the climate system, including thermometer data, glacial retreat, sea level rise, and so on. The conclusion that humans are the primary cause of this warming is supported by model-based attribution studies, empirical analyses that employ econometric-like methods, skillful model predictions, and the consistency of observed changes with expectations based on physical understanding. Coarse-grained conclusions about future changes in global temperature are supported by multiple generations of modeling results, theoretical process understanding, changes already observed to occur, and estimates of climate sensitivity that are themselves underwritten by diverse evidence from models, paleoclimate data, and so on. Often, lines of evidence are also accompanied by some form of robustness analysis that demonstrates the relative insensitivity of findings to changes in models, methods, and assumptions.

Pragmatic solutions to difficult epistemic problems. The periodic assessments of the IPCC place unusual epistemic demands on climate science. Scientists participating in these assessments are tasked with assessing and synthesizing a vast scientific literature and then communicating conclusions, as well as uncertainties, in a way that will be useful to policymakers. In response to these very difficult epistemic tasks, which moreover must be completed in a timely manner, climate scientists have developed pragmatic approaches to evidence synthesis and to uncertainty estimation and communication, which balance rigor with tractability and simplicity. We saw this, for example, in the way that a quantitative estimate of the human contribution to recent warming was reached, via a covering range over three attribution studies, and also in the "default approach" to estimating future warming from CMIP ensembles, with its Normal distribution and downgrading of likelihood. Such pragmatic methods clearly have limitations. Yet critics may be hard-pressed to find more rigorous approaches that avoid false precision and still meet the requirements of tractability and simplicity.

These features of the epistemology of climate science are unlikely to change anytime soon. But ongoing discussions and developments in the field point to other possible changes. First, as noted in Section 4, climate scientists are currently discussing (and debating) whether the field should be less uniformly oriented toward avoiding Type I error; perhaps future climate science will exhibit a more context-sensitive approach to methodological choices, guided explicitly by consideration of the stakes of error in the context at hand. Second, some climate scientists are advocating a fundamental change in the organization of climate modeling; rather than maintaining several dozen GCMs/ESMs at modeling centers around the world, they envision pooling human and computational resources to develop just a few models with very high spatial resolution (e.g., 1–10 km). Such a change might impact the epistemology of climate science in a host of subtle ways (and perhaps some not-so-subtle ones too). Finally, climate scientists are currently exploring how methods of machine learning/artificial intelligence can be fruitfully employed across the field. Depending on their level of success, these methods could become an important part of climate science in the future, adding another layer of richness and complexity to its epistemology.

References

Adams, P., Eitland, E., Hewitson, B., et al. (2015). Toward an ethical framework for climate services: A white paper of the Climate Services Partnership Working Group on Climate Services Ethics. Climate Services Partnership Paper, p. 12, www.climate-services.org/wp-content/uploads/2015/09/CS-Ethics-White-Paper-Oct-2015.pdf.

Adler, C., & Hirsch Hadorn, G. (2014). The IPCC and Treatment of Uncertainties: Topics and Sources of Dissensus. *Wiley Interdisciplinary Reviews Climate Change*, 5(5), 663–676.

Arias, P. A., Bellouin, N., Coppola, E., et al. (2021). Technical Summary. In V. Masson-Delmotte, P. Zhai, A. Pirani, et al., eds., *Climate Change 2021: The Physical Science Basis. Contribution of Working Group I to the Sixth Assessment Report of the Intergovernmental Panel on Climate Change.* Cambridge: Cambridge University Press, pp. 553–672.

Baumberger, C., Knutti, R. & Hirsch-Hadorn, G. (2017). Building Confidence in Climate Model Projections: An Analysis of Inferences from Fit. *Wiley Interdisciplinary Reviews: Climate Change*, 8, e454.

Betz, G. (2013). In Defence of the Value Free Ideal. *European Journal for Philosophy of Science*, 3(2), 207–220.

Betz, G. (2015). Are Climate Models Credible Worlds? Prospects and Limitations of Possibilistic Climate Prediction. *European Journal for Philosophy of Science*, 5(2), 191–215.

Biddle, J. B., & E. Winsberg (2010). Value Judgments and the Estimation of Uncertainty in Climate Modeling. In P. D. Magnus & J. Busch, eds., *New Waves in the Philosophy of Science*, New York: Palgrave MacMillan, pp. 172–197.

Bindoff, N. L., Stott, P. A., AchutaRao, K. M., et al. (2013). Chapter 10 – Detection and Attribution of Climate Change: From Global to Regional. In T. F. Stocker, D. Qin, G.-K. Plattner, et al., eds., *Climate Change 2013: The Physical Science Basis: Contribution of Working Group I to the Fifth Assessment Report of the Intergovernmental Panel on Climate Change.* Cambridge: Cambridge University Press, pp. 867–952.

Bokulich. A. (2017). Models and Explanation. In L. Magnani and T. Bertolotti, eds., *Handbook of Model-based Science.* Dordrecht: Springer, pp. 103–118.

Bokulich, A. (2018). Using Models to Correct Data: Paleodiversity and the Fossil Record. *Synthese*, 198, 5919–5940.

Bokulich, A. & Parker, W. S. (2021). Data Models, Representation and Adequacy-for-Purpose. *European Journal for Philosophy of Science*, 11, 31.

Bovens, L., & Hartmann, S. (2004). *Bayesian Epistemology*. Oxford: Oxford University Press.

Bradley, R., Frigg, R., Steele, K., Thompson, E., & Werndl, C. (2020). The Philosophy of Climate Science. *Internet Encyclopedia of Philosophy*. https://iep.utm.edu/. Accessed November 26, 2023.

Carrier, M. & Lenhard, J. (2019). Climate Models: How to Assess their Reliability. *International Studies in Philosophy of Science*, 32(2): 81–100.

Collins, M., Knutti, R., Arblaster, J., et al. (2013). Long-term Climate Change: Projections, Commitments and Irreversibility. In T. F. Stocker, D. Qin, G.-K. Plattner, et al., eds., *Climate Change 2013: The Physical Science Basis. Contribution of Working Group I to the Fifth Assessment Report of the Intergovernmental Panel on Climate Change*. Cambridge: Cambridge University Press, pp. 1029–1136.

Compo, G. P., Sardeshmukh, P. D., Whitaker, et al. (2013). Independent Confirmation of Global Land Warming without the Use of Station Temperatures. *Geophysical Research Letters*, 40, 3170–3174.

Cowtan, K., & Way, R.G. (2014). Coverage Bias in the HadCRUT4 Temperature Series and Its Impact on Recent Temperature Trends. *Quarterly Journal of the Royal Meteorological Society*, 140(683), 1935–1944.

Currie, A. (2018). From Models-as-Fictions to Models-as-Tools. *Ergo*, 4(27), 759–781.

Dawid, R., Hartmann, S., & Sprenger, J. (2015). The No Alternatives Argument. *The British Journal for the Philosophy of Science*, 66(1), 213–234.

Dethier, C. (2022). When is an Ensemble like a Sample? "Model-based" Inferences in Climate Modelling. *Synthese*, 200(52), 1–22.

Dethier, C. (2023a). Interpreting the Probabilistic Language in IPCC Reports. *Ergo*, 10(8), 203–225.

Dethier, C. (2023b). Against "Possibilist" Interpretations of Climate Models. *Philosophy of Science*, 90(5), 1417–1426. https://doi.org/10.1017/psa.2023.6.

Dethier, C. (2024). Contrast Classes and Agreement in Climate Modeling. *European Journal for the Philosophy of Science*, 14(14). https://doi.org/10.1007/s13194-024-00577-6.

Dietrich, F., & Spiekermann, K. (2021). Jury Theorems. *The Stanford Encyclopedia of Philosophy*. https://plato.stanford.edu/entries/jury-theorems/. Accessed September 17, 2023.

Edwards, P. N. (2010). *A Vast Machine: Computer Models, Climate Data, and the Politics of Global Warming.* Cambridge, MA: MIT Press.

Elabbar, A. (2023). Varying Evidential Standards as a Matter of Justice. *British Journal for the Philosophy of Science.* https://doi.org/10.1086/727429.

Eyring, V., Bony, S., Meehl, G. A., et al. (2016). Overview of the Coupled Model Intercomparison Project Phase 6 (CMIP6) Experimental Design and Organization. *Geoscientific Model Development,* 9, 1937–1958.

Eyring, V., Gillett, N. P., Achuta Rao, K. M., et al. (2021). Human Influence on the Climate System. In V. Masson-Delmotte, P. Zhai, A. Pirani, et al., eds., *Climate Change 2021: The Physical Science Basis. Contribution of Working Group I to the Sixth Assessment Report of the Intergovernmental Panel on Climate Change.* Cambridge: Cambridge University Press, pp. 423–552, https://doi.org/10.1017/9781009157896.005.

Folland, C. K., Boucher, O., Colman, A., & Parker, D. E. (2018) Causes of Irregularities in Trends of Global Mean Surface Temperature since the late 19th Century. *Science Advances,* 4, eaao5297.

Forster, P., Storelvmo, T., Armour, K., et al. (2021). The Earth's Energy Budget, Climate Feedbacks, and Climate Sensitivity. In V. Masson-Delmotte, P. Zhai, A. Pirani, et al., eds., *Climate Change 2021: The Physical Science Basis. Contribution of Working Group I to the Sixth Assessment Report of the Intergovernmental Panel on Climate Change.* Cambridge: Cambridge University Press, pp. 923–1054.

Frame, D. J., Faull, N. E., Joshi, M. M., & Allen, M. R. 2007. Probabilistic Climate Forecasts and Inductive Problems. *Philosophical Transactions of the Royal Society* A, 365, 1971–1992.

Frigg, R., Thompson, E., and Werndl, C. (2015a). Philosophy of Climate Science Part I: Observing Climate Change. *Philosophy Compass,* 10 (12): 953–964.

Frigg, R., Thompson, E., and Werndl, C. (2015b). Philosophy of Climate Science Part II: Modelling Climate Change. *Philosophy Compass,* 10 (12): 965–977.

Gillett, N. P., Kirchmeier-Young, M., Ribes, A., et al. (2021). Constraining Human Contributions to Observed Warming since the Pre-industrial Period. *Nature Climate Change,* 11(3), 207–212.

Gleckler, P. J., Taylor, K. E., & Doutriaux, C. (2008) Performance Metrics for Climate Models. *Journal of Geophysical Research,* 113, D06104.

Gulev, S. K., Thorne, P. W., Ahn, J., et al. (2021). Changing State of the Climate System. In V. Masson-Delmotte, P. Zhai, A. Pirani, et al., eds., *Climate Change 2021: The Physical Science Basis. Contribution of Working Group*

I to the Sixth Assessment Report of the Intergovernmental Panel on Climate Change. New York: Cambridge University Press, pp. 287–422.

Hall, A., & Qu, X. (2006). Using the Current Seasonal Cycle to Constrain Snow Albedo Feedback in Future Climate Change. *Geophysical Research Letters,* 33, L03502.

Hansen, J. E., & Lebedeff, S. (1987). Global Trends of Measured Surface Air Temperature. *Journal of Geophysical Research,* 92, 13345–13372.

Harris, M. (2021) *Conceptualizing Uncertainty: The IPCC, Model Robustness and the Weight of Evidence.* PhD Thesis, The London School of Economics. https://etheses.lse.ac.uk/4355/1/Harris__Conceptualizing-uncertainty-IPCC-model-robustness.pdf.

Harris, T. (2003). Data Models and the Acquisition and Manipulation of Data. *Philosophy of Science,* 70(5), 1508–1517.

Hartmann, D. L., Klein Tank, A. M. G., Rusticucci, M., et al. (2013). Observations: Atmosphere and Surface. In T. F. Stocker, D. Qin, G.-K. Plattner, et al., eds., *Climate Change 2013: The Physical Science Basis. Contribution of Working Group I to the Fifth Assessment Report of the Intergovernmental Panel on Climate Change.* Cambridge: Cambridge University Press, pp. 159–254.

Hausfather, Z. (2017). Analysis: How well have climate models projected global warming? www.carbonbrief.org/analysis-how-well-have-climate-models-projected-global-warming/. Accessed December 5, 2023.

Haustein, K., Allen, M. R., Forster, P. M., et al. (2017). A Real-Time Global Warming Index. *Scientific Reports,* 7(1), 15417.

Hazeleger, W., van den Hurk, B. J. J. M., Min, E., et al. (2015). Tales of Future Weather. *Nature Climate Change,* 5, 107–113.

Hegerl, G. C., Zwiers, F. W., Braconnot, P., et al. (2007). Understanding and Attributing Climate Change. In S. Solomon, D. Qin, M. Manning, et al., eds., *Climate Change 2007: The Physical Science Basis. Contribution of Working Group I to the Fourth Assessment Report of the Intergovernmental Panel on Climate Change.* Cambridge: Cambridge University Press, pp. 663–745.

Heinze, C., Eyring, V., Friedlingstein, P., et al. (2019). Climate Feedbacks in the Earth System and Prospects for their Evaluation. *Earth System Dynamics,* 10, 379–452.

Huber, M., & Knutti, R. (2014). Natural Variability, Radiative Forcing and Climate Response in the Recent Hiatus Reconciled. *Nature Geoscience,* 7, 651–656.

Intemann, K. (2015). Distinguishing Between Legitimate and Illegitimate Values in Climate Modeling. *European Journal for Philosophy of Science,* 5(2), 217–232.

IPCC. (2013). Summary for Policymakers. In T. F. Stocker, D. Qin, G.-K. Plattner, et al., eds., *Climate Change 2013: The Physical Science Basis. Contribution of Working Group I to the Fifth Assessment Report of the Intergovernmental Panel on Climate Change*. Cambridge: Cambridge University Press, pp. 3–29.

IPCC. (2021). *Climate Change 2021: The Physical Science Basis. Contribution of Working Group I to the Sixth Assessment Report of the Intergovernmental Panel on Climate Change*. V. Masson-Delmotte, P. Zhai, A. Pirani, et al., eds., Cambridge: Cambridge University Press.

IPCC (2023). *Climate Change 2023: Synthesis Report. Contribution of Working Groups I, II and III to the Sixth Assessment Report of the Intergovernmental Panel on Climate Change*. Core Writing Team, H. Lee and J. Romero, eds., Geneva, Switzerland: IPCC.

Jebeile, J., & Crucifix, M. (2020). Multi-Model Ensembles in Climate Science: Mathematical Structures and Expert Judgements. *Studies in History and Philosophy of Science Part A*, 83, 44–52.

Jebeile, J., & Crucifix, M. (2021). Value Management and Model Pluralism in Climate Science. *Studies in History and Philosophy of Science Part A*, 88, 120–127.

Jebeile, J., & Graham Kennedy, A. (2015). Explaining with Models: The Role of Idealizations. *International Studies in the Philosophy of Science*, 29(4), 383–392.

John, S. (2015). The Example of the IPCC Does Not Vindicate the Value Free Ideal: A Reply to Gregor Betz. *European Journal for Philosophy of Science*, 5(1), 1–13.

John, S. (2016). From Social Values to P-Values: The Social Epistemology of the Intergovernmental Panel on Climate Change. *Journal of Applied Philosophy*, 34(2), 157–171.

Kawamleh, S. (2022). Confirming (Climate) Change: A Dynamical Account of Model Evaluation. *Synthese*, 200(2), 1–26.

Katzav, J. (2013). Severe Testing of Climate Change Hypotheses. *Studies in History and Philosophy of Modern Physics*, 44(4), 433–441.

Katzav, J. (2014). The Epistemology of Climate Models and Some of Its Implications for Climate Science and the Philosophy of Science. *Studies in History and Philosophy of Modern Physics*, 46(2), 228–238.

Katzav, J., & Parker, W. S. (2018). Issues in the Theoretical Foundations of Climate Science. *Studies in History and Philosophy of Modern Physics*, 63, 141–149.

Katzav, J., Thompson, E. L., Risbey, J., et al. (2021). On the Appropriate and Inappropriate Uses of Probability Distributions in Climate Projections and Some Alternatives. *Climatic Change*, 169(15).

Kennedy, J. J., Rayner, N. A., Atkinson, C. P., & Killick, R. E. (2019). An Ensemble Data Set of Sea Surface Temperature Change from 1850: The Met Office Hadley Centre HadSST.4.0.0.0 Data Set. *Journal of Geophysical Research – Atmospheres*, 124(14), 7719–7763.

Knutti, R. (2010). The End of Model Democracy? *Climatic Change*, 102, 395–404.

Knutti, R. (2018). Climate Model Confirmation: From Philosophy to Predicting Climate in the Real World. In E. A. Lloyd and E. Winsberg, eds., *Climate Modelling*. Cham: Palgrave Macmillan.

Knutti, R., & Sedláček, J. (2013). Robustness and Uncertainties in the New CMIP5 Climate Model Projections. *Nature Climate Change*, 3, 369–373.

Knutti, R., Sedláček, J., Sanderson, B. M., et al. (2017). A Climate Model Projection Weighting Scheme Accounting for Performance and Interdependence. *Geophysical Research Letters*, 44(4), 1909–1918.

Knutson, T., Camargo, S. J., Chan, J. C. L., et al. (2019). Tropical Cyclones and Climate Change Assessment: Part I: Detection and Attribution. *Bulletin of the American Meteorological Society*, 100(10), 1987–2007.

Knuuttila, T. (2011). Modeling and Representing: An Artifactual Approach. *Studies in History and Philosophy of Science A*, 42(2), 262–71.

Kosaka, Y., & Xie, S. P. (2013). Recent Global-Warming Hiatus Tied to Equatorial Pacific Surface Cooling. *Nature*, 501, 403–407.

Lam, V., & Majszak, M. (2022). Climate Tipping Points and Expert Judgment. *WIREs Climate Change*, 13(6), e805.

Lee, J. (2021). *On non-epistemic values in climate science for decision support*. PhD Thesis, University of Cape Town. http://hdl.handle.net/11427/35896.

Lee, J.-Y., Marotzke, J., Bala, G., et al. (2021). Future Global Climate: Scenario-Based Projections and Near-Term Information. In V. Masson-Delmotte, P. Zhai, A. Pirani, et al., eds., *Climate Change 2021: The Physical Science Basis. Contribution of Working Group I to the Sixth Assessment Report of the Intergovernmental Panel on Climate Change*. Cambridge: Cambridge University Press, pp. 553–672, https://doi.org/10.1017/9781009157896.006.

Lenhard, J., & Winsberg, E. (2010). Holism, Entrenchment, and the Future of Climate Model Pluralism. *Studies in History and Philosophy of Modern Physics*, 41(3), 253–262.

Lenssen, N., Schmidt, G. A., Hansen, J. E., et al. (2019). Improvements in the GISTEMP Uncertainty Model. *Journal of Geophysical Research: Atmospheres*, 124(12), 6307–6326.

Leonelli, S. (2019). What Distinguishes Data from Models? *European Journal for Philosophy of Science*, 9, 22.

Leuschner, A. (2015). Uncertainties, Plurality, and Robustness in Climate Research and Modeling: On the Reliability of Climate Prognoses. *Journal for General Philosophy of Science*, 46, 367–381.

Liang, Y., Gillett, N. P., & Monahan, A. H. (2020). Climate Model Projections of 21st Century Global Warming Constrained Using the Observed Warming Trend. *Geophysical Research Letters*, 47(12), e2019GL086757.

Lloyd, E. A. (2015). Model Robustness as a Confirmatory Virtue: The Case of Climate Science. *Studies in History and Philosophy of Science Part A*, 49, 58–68.

Lloyd, E. A. & Oreskes, N. (2018). Climate Change Attribution: When Is It Appropriate to Accept New Methods? *Earth's Future*, 6(3), 311–325.

Lloyd, E. A. & Winsberg, E., eds., (2018). *Climate Modelling*. Cham: Palgrave Macmillan.

Lloyd, E. A., Oreskes, N., Seneviratne, S. I., & Larson, E. J. (2021). Climate Scientists Set the Bar of Proof Too High. *Climatic Change*, 165, 55. https://doi.org/10.1007/s10584-021-03061-9.

Lorenz, E. N. (1970). Climatic Change as a Mathematical Problem. *Journal of Applied Meteorology*, 9(3), 325–329.

Masson, D., & Knutti, R. (2011). Climate Model Genealogy. *Geophysical Research Letters*, 38, L08703.

Mastrandrea, M. D., Mach, K. J., Plattner, G.-K., et al. (2011). The IPCC AR5 Guidance Note on Consistent Treatment of Uncertainties: A Common Approach across the Working Groups. *Climatic Change*, 108, 675.

Mayo, D. (1996). *Error and the Growth of Experimental Knowledge*. Chicago: Chicago University Press.

Mayo, D. (2018). *Statistical Inference as Severe Testing*. Cambridge: Cambridge University Press.

Meehl, G. A., Arblaster, J. M., Fasullo, J. T., Hu, A., & Trenberth, K. E. (2011). Model-Based Evidence of Deep-Ocean Heat Uptake during Surface-Temperature Hiatus Periods. *Nature Climate Change*, 1, 360–364.

Morice, C. P., Kennedy, J. J., Rayner, N. A., et al. (2021). An Updated Assessment of Near-Surface Temperature Change from 1850: The HadCRUT5 Dataset. *Journal of Geophysical Research: Atmospheres*, 126(3), e2019JD032361.

Muller, R. A., Wurtele, J., Rohde, R., et al. (2013). Earth Atmospheric Land Surface Temperature and Station Quality in the Contiguous United States. *Geoinformatics and Geostatistics: An Overview*, 1(3).

Odenbaugh, J. (2018). Building Trust, Removing Doubt? Robustness Analysis and Climate Modeling. In E. A. Lloyd & E. Winsberg, eds., *Climate Modelling: Philosophical and Conceptual Issues*. Cham: Springer Verlag. pp. 297–321.

O'Loughlin, R. (2021). Robustness Reasoning in Climate Model Comparisons. *Studies in History and Philosophy of Science Part* A, 85(C), 34–43.

Parker, W. S. (2006). Understanding Pluralism in Climate Modeling. *Foundations of Science*, 11(4), 349–368.

Parker, W. S. (2009). Confirmation and Adequacy-for-Purpose in Climate Modeling. *Aristotelian Society Supplementary Volume*, 83, 233–249.

Parker, W. S. (2010). Whose Probabilities? Predicting Climate Change with Ensembles of Models. *Philosophy of Science*, 77(5), 985–997.

Parker, W. S. (2011). When Climate Models Agree: The Significance of Robust Model Predictions. *Philosophy of Science*, 78(4), 579–600.

Parker, W. S. (2017). Computer Simulation, Measurement and Data Assimilation. *The British Journal for the Philosophy of Science*, 68(1), 273–304.

Parker, W. S. (2018). Climate Science. In E. N. Zalta & U. Nodelman, eds., *Stanford Encyclopedia of Philosophy* (Fall 2023 Edition). https://plato.stanford.edu/archives/fall2023/entries/climate-science/.

Parker, W. S. (2020). Model Evaluation: An Adequacy-for-Purpose View. *Philosophy of Science*, 87(3), 457–477.

Parker, W. S. (2021). Virtually a Measurement. *Nature Physics*, 17, 146.

Parker, W. S., & Risbey, J. S. (2015). False Precision, Surprise and Improved Uncertainty Assessment. *Philosophical Transactions of the Royal Society, Part A*, 373(3055), 20140453.

Parker, W. S., & Winsberg, E. (2018). Values and Evidence: How Models Make a Difference. *European Journal for Philosophy of Science*, 8(1), 125–142.

Pennell, C., & Reichler, T. (2011). On the Effective Number of Climate Models. *Journal of Climate*, 24(9), 2358–2367.

Phillips, N. (1956). The General Circulation of the Atmosphere: A Numerical Experiment. *Quarterly Journal of the Royal Meteorological Society*, 82(352), 123–164.

Pirtle, Z., Meyer, R., & Hamilton, A. (2010), What Does it Mean When Climate Models Agree? A Case for Assessing Independence among General Circulation Models. *Environmental Science & Policy*, 13(5), 351–361.

Pulkkinen, K., Undorf, S., Bender, F., et al. (2022). The Value of Values in Climate Science. *Nature Climate Change*, 12, 4–6.

Rehg, W., & Staley, K. (2017). "Agreement" in the IPCC Confidence Measure. *Studies in History and Philosophy of Modern Physics*, 57, 126–134

Reiss, J. (2015). A Pragmatist Theory of Evidence. *Philosophy of Science*, 82, 341–362.

Ribes, A., Qasmi, S., & Gillett, N. P. (2021). Making Climate Projections Conditional on Historical Observations. *Science Advances*, 7(4), eabc0671.

Risbey, J. S. 2007. Subjective Elements in Climate Policy Advice. *Climatic Change*, 85(1), 11–17.

Risbey, J. S., Lewandowsky, S., Langlais, C., et al. (2014). Well-Estimated Global Surface Warming in Climate Projections Selected for ENSO Phase. *Nature Climate Change*, 4, 835–840.

Rohde, R., Muller, R., Jacobsen, R., et al. (2013). Berkeley Earth Temperature Averaging Process. *Geoinformatics and Geostatistics: An Overview*, 1(2), https://doi.org/10.4172/gigs.1000103.

Schmidt, G. (2013). The IPCC AR5 Attribution Statement. Realclimate.org. www.realclimate.org/index.php/archives/2013/10/the-ipcc-ar5-attribution-statement/. Accessed 30 November 2023.

Schmidt, G., Shindell, D., & Tsigaridis, K. (2014). Reconciling Warming Trends. *Nature Geoscience*, 7, 158–160.

Schmidt, G., & Sherwood, S. (2015). A Practical Philosophy of Complex Climate Modelling. *European Journal for Philosophy of Science*, 5(2), 149–169.

Schupbach, J. N. (2018). Robustness Analysis as Explanatory Reasoning. *The British Journal for the Philosophy of Science*, 69(1), 275–300.

Shepherd, T. G. (2019). Storyline Approach to the Construction of Regional Climate Change Information. *Proceedings of the Royal Society A*, 475, 20190013.

Sherwood, S. C., Webb, M. J., Annan, J. D., et al. (2020). An Assessment of Earth's Climate Sensitivity Using Multiple Lines of Evidence. *Reviews of Geophysics*, 58(4), e2019RG000678.

Smith, L. A. (2002). What Might We Learn from Climate Forecasts? *Proceedings of the National Academies of Science*, 99(Supp 1), 2487–2492.

Stainforth, D. A., Allen, M. R., Tredger, E. R., & Smith, L. A. (2007). Confidence, Uncertainty and Decision-Support Relevance in Climate Predictions. *Philosophical Transactions of the Royal Society A*, 365, 2145–61.

Steele, K. S. (2012). The Scientist qua Policy Advisor Makes Value Judgments. *Philosophy of Science*, 79(5), 893–904.

Stolpe, M. B., Medhaug, I., & Knutti, R. (2017). Contribution of Atlantic and Pacific Multidecadal Variability to Twentieth-Century Temperature Changes. *Journal of Climate*, 30(16), 6279–6295.

Suppes, P. (1962). Models of Data. In E. Nagel, P. Suppes, and A. Tarski, eds., *Logic, Methodology, and Philosophy of Science: Proceedings of the 1960*

International Congress. Stanford, CA: Stanford University Press, pp. 252–261.

Susskind, J., Schmidt, G. A., Lee, J. N., & Iredell, L. (2019). Recent Global Warming as Confirmed by AIRS. *Environmental Research Letters*, 14(4), 044030.

Tal, E. (2012). *The Epistemology of Measurement: A Model-Based Approach.* PhD dissertation, University of Toronto.

Tal, E. (2017). A Model-Based Epistemology of Measurement. In N. Mößner & A. Nordmann, eds., *Reasoning in Measurement.* London: Routledge, pp. 233–253.

Thompson, E., Frigg, R. & Helgeson, C. (2016). Expert Judgment for Climate Change Adaptation. *Philosophy of Science*, 83(5), 1110–1121.

Thorne, P. W., Trewin, B., Allan, R. P., et al. (2021). Cross-Chapter Box 2.3: New Estimates of Global Warming to Date, and Key Implications. In Masson-Delmotte, V., P. Zhai, A. Pirani, et al., eds., *Climate Change 2021: The Physical Science Basis. Contribution of Working Group I to the Sixth Assessment Report of the Intergovernmental Panel on Climate Change.* Cambridge: Cambridge University Press, pp. 317–323, https://doi.org/10.1017/9781009157896.006.

Tokarska, K. B., Stolpe, M. B., Stippel, S., et al. (2020). Past Warming Trend Constrains Future Warming in CMIP6 Models. *Science Advances*, 6(12), aaz9549.

Undorf, S., Pulkkinen, K., Wikman-Svahn, P., & Bender, F., A.-M. (2022). How Do Value-Judgements Enter Model-Based Assessments of Climate Sensitivity? *Climatic Change*, 174, 19.

van Fraassen, B. C. (2008). *Scientific Representation.* Oxford: Oxford University Press.

Vezér, M. A. (2017). Variety-of-Evidence Reasoning about the Distant Past: A Case Study in Paleoclimate Reconstruction. *European Journal for Philosophy of Science*, 7(2), 257–265.

Voosen, P. (2021). Climate Panel Confronts Implausibly Hot Models. *Science*, 373(6554), 474–475.

Watkins, A. (2024). Using Paleoclimate Analogues to Inform Climate Projections. *Perspectives on Science.* https://doi.org/10.1162/posc_a_00622.

Weart, S. (2023). Climatology as a Profession. https://history.aip.org/climate/climogy.htm. Accessed September 17, 2023.

Weigel, A. P., Knutti, R., Liniger, M. A., & Appenzeller, C. (2010). Risks of Model Weighting in Multimodel Climate Projections. *Journal of Climate*, 23(15), 4175–4191.

Werndl, C. (2016). On Defining Climate and Climate Change. *British Journal for the Philosophy of Science*, 67(2), 337–364.

Wilson, J., & Boudinot, F. G. (2022). Proxy Measurement in Paleoclimatology. *European Journal for Philosophy of Science*, 12(1), 14.

Winsberg, E. (2012). Values and Uncertainties in the Predictions of Global Climate Models. *Kennedy Institute of Ethics Journal*, 22(2), 111–137.

Winsberg, E. (2018a). *Philosophy and Climate Science*. Cambridge: Cambridge University Press.

Winsberg, E. (2018b). Communicating Uncertainty to Policymakers: The Ineliminable Role of Values. In E. A. Lloyd & E. Winsberg, eds., *Climate Modelling*. Cham: Palgrave Macmillan. https://doi.org/10.1007/978-3-319-65058-6_13.

Zelinka, M., Myers, T. A., McCoy, D. T., et al. (2020). Causes of Higher Climate Sensitivity in CMIP6 Models. *Geophysical Research Letters*, 47(1), e2019GL085782.

Acknowledgments

Thanks to Lenny Smith, Gavin Schmidt, Corey Dethier, and Deborah Mayo for helpful feedback on the draft manuscript. I am also grateful for many discussions over the years with Alisa Bokulich, Eric Winsberg, and Joel Katzav, which in various ways informed and shaped ideas in this book. Some material in Section 2 is based on work supported by the US National Science Foundation under Grant No. SES-1127710.

Cambridge Elements ☰

Philosophy of Science

Jacob Stegenga
University of Cambridge

Jacob Stegenga is a Reader in the Department of History and Philosophy of Science at the University of Cambridge. He has published widely on fundamental topics in reasoning and rationality and philosophical problems in medicine and biology. Prior to joining Cambridge he taught in the United States and Canada, and he received his PhD from the University of California San Diego.

About the Series

This series of Elements in Philosophy of Science provides an extensive overview of the themes, topics and debates which constitute the philosophy of science. Distinguished specialists provide an up-to-date summary of the results of current research on their topics, as well as offering their own take on those topics and drawing original conclusions.

Cambridge Elements ≡

Philosophy of Science

Printed in the United States
by Baker & Taylor Publisher Services